LEADERSHIP IS A
BEHAVIOR NOT A TITLE

LEADERSHIP IS A BEHAVIOR NOT A TITLE

YOUR POCKET GUIDE TO
BEING A LEADER WORTH FOLLOWING

DDS DOBSON-SMITH

LIONCREST
PUBLISHING

LEADERSHIP IS A BEHAVIOR NOT A TITLE

Your Pocket Guide to Being a Leader Worth Following

FIRST EDITION

ISBN 978-1-5445-3555-5 *Paperback*

978-1-5445-3556-2 *Ebook*

I would like to dedicate this book to some important people: the leaders I have followed or been inspired by over the years of my professional career.

Each of you has contributed to this book, and to my life, in ways that I hope you will see and ways in which you may never know. I am forever grateful and indebted to each of you:

Abbey Whitney, Adam Russell, Amanda Schmidt, Alex Crowther, Amari Pocock, Angelique Gilmer, Anu Singh, Anna Benassi, Andrew Shebbeare, Andy Bonsall, Andy Mitchell CBE, Angela Toon, Anne Molignano, Brandon Friesen, Brian Krick, Carol-Ann White, Cathy Carl, Chris Sexton, Christian Juhl, CJ Johnson, Claire Libbey, Danielle Sporkin, Dave Marsey, David Allen, Davis Dobson-Smith, Dawn Barker, DeAngela Black-Cooks, Emily Marinelli, Emma Harris, Eric Perko, Evan Hanlon, Gabe Miller, Dr George Kitahara-Kich, Iain Niven-Bowling, Ian Nunn, Jack Swayne, Jason Harrison, Jane Geraghty, Jennifer Remling, Jeremy Sigel, Jo Ascough, Joe Parente, Jude McCormack, Katie Mancini, Keith Hatter, Kishan Unarket, Kunal Guha, Kyoko Matsushita, Llibert Argerich, Liv Bernardini, Matt Isaacs, Marc Noaro, Mark Nancarrow, Mimi Chakrovorty, Neil Cummings, Nick Byrd, Nicolas Petrovic, Paul Smith, Peter Guagenti, Rachel Brace, Rhi Watkins, Rich Mooney, Richard Brown CBE, Richard George, Richard Hartell, Rob Reifenheiser, Sarah Potemkin, Sarah Walker, Sharon Pavitt, Sherwin Su, Simmone Page, Steve Williams, Taunya Black-Cooks, Thomas Ellingson, Thomas Ordahl, Tim Irwin, Tony Rafetto, Tony Santabarbara, Tricia Wright, Valerie Todd, Vicki Williams, and Veli Aghdiran.

CONTENTS

INTRODUCTION

My first crisis of confidence in my work life came shortly after I started working.

I was a college professor in the UK and, in fact, I was the *youngest* college professor in the UK at the time. I taught hospitality management, and one of my courses was on public house operations. There was a mature student in that class named Howard who was born on the same day in the same year as my mum. He had owned his own pub longer than I had been alive. As I handed Howard an assignment that I had graded with a C, I caught a look in his eyes, and I thought to myself, *This doesn't feel right*. I was doing my job as a college professor, and yet something about it just didn't sit well with me.

So, I decided that I would go out into the world and get more life experience under my belt, telling myself I would eventually return to academia. I searched the job market for jobs in human resources (or personnel management as it was called back then), because I thought that was as close as possible to academia while being in the corporate world. And I got a job with Marks & Spencer, the British retailer, as a personnel management trainee.

In one of the stores I worked in, I had to manage a woman named Diana who had been a personnel supervisor for twenty-five years. Meanwhile, I had only been a trainee for six months. Instantly it felt like the situation with Howard, the mature student in my class, was repeating itself.

Here I was again in a position of hierarchical power with this brilliant woman who was old enough to be my mother and who had been doing her job for twenty-five years. What the hell did I have to offer her?

In that moment, I suffered another crisis of confidence, the second coming so soon on the heels of the first.

I went to my manager, Simmone Page, who was head

of HR for the store, and asked her, "What should I do? I can't tell someone my mum's age how to do her job!"

Simmone kindly said to me, "No, you can't possibly tell her how to do her job from a management perspective, but you *can* be there for her. You can create the conditions for her to be successful. You can remove the roadblocks that are in the way, and you can use your position to make things easier for her to do her job. You can believe in her. You can help her when she's having a hard day."

She took a beat before continuing. "Stop trying to master the technicalities of her job, because that's not your job. Your job here is to be a leader."

That was the moment when I had to begin letting go of my own ego.

And that conversation started to sow the seeds that have grown into this book you now hold in your hands.

LEADERSHIP VERSUS MANAGEMENT

A lot of us carry around this idea in our heads that if we are in a leadership position, we have to know all the answers. And we have to have the *right* answers; we can't get things wrong. We have to be the paragons of virtue, or we have to "know best," as it were.

In actuality, the opposite is true. If we want to create spaces where people can be their best, where they can feel like they belong, and where they can have their energy released to do great work, then it's not about being a manager. It's about being a leader.

But what does that mean, really? What is the difference between leadership and management? (A difference which, as the title of this section would suggest, does exist.) Let's first look at what being a leader is *not*.

A 2018 article in *Forbes* shares a statistic that highlights the real crisis in leadership.[1] Drawing from a 2016 Gallup poll, the author of the article identified that 82 percent of managers and executives are seen as lacking in leadership skills by their employees. This means that employees report that *more than three-quarters of all managers* do not do a great job of leading them. Gallup also estimated that this lack of leadership capability was costing US corporations alone up to $550 billion annually.

---

1   Hougaard, "The Real Crisis in Leadership."

The article also goes on to quote a report from Deloitte, which approximated that $46 billion is being spent annually on leadership-development programs around the globe—which *are not working.*

Leadership training is failing. And why is it failing? Well, likely because it's trying to teach the wrong things. As Javier Pladevall, the CEO of Volkswagen Spain, has said, "Leadership today is about unlearning management and relearning being human."

That's why I wrote this book—because the world is wasting money on trying to create great leaders instead of trying to create great humans. It's not enough for a leader to talk about their good intentions. They have to place equal attention on their impact as they do their intentions. Showing up and behaving like a decent human being is what is going to turn this crisis around.

HOW DID WE GET HERE?

In 2021, we saw the beginnings of what has since been termed the Great Resignation—a serious uptake in resignations across the US—and in fact around the world. With everything that's happened since early 2020—the pandemic and the social justice crises we've been experiencing—people have been asking themselves some deep, existential questions.

From a professional perspective, people ask, "Am I doing what I want to do? I'm spending time breaking my back, potentially putting myself at risk, and making sacrifices to earn a salary. Is it paying off?"

For many people, the answer to that question has been no, and so they have gotten off the treadmill and either changed careers or stopped working.

For many other people, the answer has been, "Yes, I am doing what I want to do, and it is worth it." So the next question they ask themselves is, "Am I doing it *where* I want to?" They then turn their minds to their employers and consider, "Am I experiencing a workplace that gives me purpose and work that is meaningful? Do I feel like I belong here?"

The people who don't currently experience that purpose, meaning, and belonging are going to find places to work where they do experience them.

Everyone talks about a "shortage of talent," but I think that's bunkum. There isn't a shortage of talent; there's just a greater amount of *discernment* among the talent. And the companies that are going to win out in this new world of employment are the ones that are going to offer purpose, meaning, and belonging.

With that established, guess which person has the most influence over whether an employee experiences purpose, meaning, and belonging in their workplace?

That's correct; it's their manager.

One of the crucial findings of the vast piece of research that led to *First, Break All the Rules: What the World's Greatest Managers Do Differently*, the 1999 book by Marcus Buckingham and Curt Coffman, two researchers from the Gallup organization, is that people don't leave bad companies; they leave bad managers. You could work for a truly terrible company—any corporation that doesn't have the best reputation in the marketplace—but if you're working underneath a manager who treats you the way you want to be treated (using the six principles of human leadership, which we will talk about in much greater detail), then you are likely to want to stay at that organization, to commit to it, to show up, and to perform and deliver.

The converse is also true. You could be working for a company that embodies all the ideals that you want to put out into the world and shares your values, but if the manager of your specific team, the person whom you interact with most directly, is not using good management practices to create the conditions for you to be successful, none of the rest of it matters.

ALL WHO MANAGE CAN LEAD, BUT YOU DON'T HAVE TO BE A MANAGER TO BE A LEADER

While there is an important distinction to make between managing and leading, there isn't necessarily as much of a distinction between being a manager and being a leader.

When many people in the world of business think of the word *leader*, they imagine somebody in a senior position, at the top of the org chart, a VP or higher. And when they think of a manager, they are thinking of someone who is more tactical, more frontline, more in the trenches.

I don't believe this to be true, because I believe that leadership is *relational*, not hierarchical.

I believe if you have a follower, you are a leader. That means you don't need the title of manager to be a leader. If you're influencing someone's work and direction of travel, and they are open to that influence and they're following you, then you are a leader.

With that established, the difference between leadership and management is that managing is about making sure things are being done right, and leadership is about doing the right thing. A manager has more tactical, day-to-day, task-focused duties, while leadership is much more behavioral. Management is about *doing*; leadership is about *being*.

When you're thinking about leadership, it is about how an individual shows up rather than about what they are doing in terms of task-focused work around the supervision of other people. No matter where you are in an organization, if you have somebody reporting to you on an org chart or as part of a RASCI,[2] you have management duties to perform: helping someone to prioritize, managing someone's performance, talking to them about their development, having weekly one-

---

2   RASCI stands for Responsible, Accountable, Supporting, Consulted, Involved. It is a framework used widely within business environments to ensure full and proper decision-making and successful delivery of work.

on-ones with them, and giving them feedback. That's managing; that's *what* you do. But leadership is about *how* you do it.

That said, you can be a manager without being a leader (as is evidenced by 82 percent of managers being seen as lacking in leadership skills.) It is entirely possible to hold the position of VP or CEO without thinking about your impact on other people, or about how to take your people on a journey, how to role model the right behaviors, how to generate motivation by articulating a why, or about operating through "supporting lines" versus "reporting lines." Just because someone is in the job with that senior title doesn't necessarily make them a leader.

Being a leader is about closing the gap between intention and behavior. The people in those management positions may have the *intention* of leading, but if their behavior isn't actually demonstrating leadership, they are not leaders. Again, leaders think about impact in equal proportion to thinking about intentions. Leadership closes the gap between intention and impact.

We can always mean well, but if we don't slow down to consider how our words, decisions, and behaviors impact those around us, we run the risk of doing some serious harm. But when you make the impact just as important as your intention, you will see how your relationships change. If leadership is also relational and nonhierarchical, then everything rests on the quality of the relationship you have with the people you want to have follow you.

MY STORY

That moment I told you about in opening the book— when I got advice from Simmone about working with Diana at Marks & Spencer in the UK—while important, was not the moment that the clouds parted, the sun shone down, and cherubs started dancing around my head. I was not fully awakened nor was I changed in that instant.

My lessons about leadership have continued. I have made some mistakes, and I've gotten some things wrong. But what I have been able to do over the years— which did start in that moment—is to slowly but surely allow my ego to recede to the background so I can become increasingly useful as an instrument for the people I lead.

In my career, I've had direct accountability over a

team as large as forty people, but then I've also been in C-suite-level positions whereby I was leading more influentially and inferentially across a group of several thousand people around the world.

Over the course of my career so far, I have seen exactly what was outlined in the *Forbes* article I mentioned earlier: employees increasingly despondent about the relationship they had with their managers. I saw people in leadership positions believing that leadership was a task instead of a behavior. And I saw companies spending so many dollars putting their people through leadership training without seeing a real return on that investment.

When I realized that I'd reached a place in my career where I felt I had gathered enough of the right skills, qualifications, experience, and outlook to be able to offer something into that space, I created a company determined to change what I saw.

I also wrote a bestselling book called *You Can Be Yourself Here*, which is about how to create inclusive workplaces using the psychology of belonging. That concept of inclusion is brought forward into this book, because it is the behavior of the people in leadership positions, in management positions, that is going to be the make or break between stagnating and moving toward a climate of inclusion. This book is called *Leadership Is a Behavior, Not a Title*, and leaders need to be able to show up and use inclusive behaviors so that inclusion actually manifests into a lived experience.

If you manage other people and want to do so in a way that is going to feel good for the people you are managing, if you want to create a climate of belonging, and if you want to improve business results in key people metrics, then the single most important factor is the way you show up and behave as a leader.

Even though I'm writing a book about leadership, I do not believe myself to be a finished product. Nor do I believe myself to be a paragon of virtue that other people should emulate. I'm just a human, with everything that comes with that—flawed, broken, winging it. This book contains the lessons I learned as I matured in my career, as I occupied increasingly senior positions, and as I came to lead more and more people.

The most important thing I have learned to do is to place the things you are going to read about in this book—the importance of self-awareness, self-acceptance, and self-development, as well as the six principles of human leadership—at the top of my list, so I can increasingly be what I'm needed to be for the people I'm leading, so they can be as successful as possible.

YOU CAN'T CHOOSE YOUR MANAGER, BUT YOU DO CHOOSE YOUR LEADER[3]

Twenty years ago, when I was working as the head of organizational development at Eurostar International, I was tasked with implementing a management development program that would help managers—at all levels—excel at the delivery of the task-focused aspects of their management role as well as the relational aspects.[4]

It was during this time when I came across a *Harvard Business Review* article published in the year 2000 by

---

3   I would like to acknowledge and thank Christopher Becker, a participant in a leadership growth workshop I was running in 2019, for the title of this section. He shared these words by explaining his learning and key takeaway at the end of a workshop in which we started to explore the tenet that leadership is a behavior, not a title.

4   Note: Some people would refer to these as the "hard" and "soft" aspects, but on the basis that these so-called soft skills—and the graceful, fluent, and fluid application of them—are the key to the door of being a leader worth following, I will never refer to them as soft.

Robert Goffee and Gareth Jones entitled "Why Should Anyone Be Led by You?" In the article (and their subsequent book of the same title, published in 2006), they share a perspective that leadership is relational and nonhierarchical. As someone who was in what I referred to as "my first grown-up job," I was both relieved and inspired by this notion. It set me on a path of discovery, research, and practice that led, two decades later, to the development of a key principle underpinning the work I do with leaders (and the title of this book)—*Leadership Is a Behavior, Not a Title.*

This principle recognizes that leadership has absolutely nothing to do with your pay grade and absolutely everything to do with the extent to which, when you look around, you have followers. And not just any followers—followers who believe in you and the direction of travel you want to take them.

The primary question I often get asked when I share this principle with leaders is, "Well, how do I get or keep followers?" My answer is an amalgam of thinking from thought leaders such as Robert Goffee and Gareth Jones, Brené Brown, Cy Wakeman, Frances Frei, Daniel Goleman, Stephen Covey, Byron Katie, and Simon Sinek, which is to guide them to bring their full

Selves[5] to their leadership role—that is, with increasing amounts of empathy, skill, and choice. When leaders bring their full Selves with increasing amounts of skill and behavioral flexibility to their work, they give permission and pave the way for others to do so as well.

So the real question you should be asking yourself isn't, "How do I become a great leader?" but, **"How do I become someone worth following?"**

The short answer is **be a decent human being**—you know, the kind of human that younger you would want to be around. Children, in general, tend to have a stronger relationship with their intuition than adults do. They pay more attention to their internal world and senses. Adults tend to be good at rationalizing and cognition, whereas kids are often more discerning about who they feel safe and secure around.

If you're unsure what, exactly, it means to be a decent human being, think of it as being the *you* that you needed when you were younger. Know that you can be a decent person, one who is empathetic and kind, who will nurture relationships, respect boundaries,

---

5   The capital S on the word "Self" is deliberate and speaks to a body of work by Heinz Kohut called *self psychology*, which is explored in my first book.

and honor your truth. Be the you who, instead of telling younger you to shut up and go to school when you've got a tummy ache, is going to believe you, stay home with you, and bring you ginger ale while you're lying on the couch.

Many people laugh at the simplicity of the statement "be a decent human being," but as we know, *simple* doesn't always mean *easy*.

HOW TO BECOME SOMEONE WORTH FOLLOWING

My longer answer to the question, "How do I become a leader worth following?" is crystallized in the remaining pages of this book, which is broken into two parts. Part I looks at the tools you can use to improve self-awareness, self-acceptance, and self-development, and Part II lays out the Six Principles of Human Leadership.

Anyone can be a leader worth following. The information here doesn't apply only to people at certain levels of leadership or only to people in America; in fact, these practices and principles have been applied globally to people in all different positions and levels of roles.

I am not espousing skills, capabilities, and qualities that are solely for the privileged, or only for people who have an Ivy League education. These skills, approaches, and outlooks are accessible and available to *anyone*, no matter where they're born, when they were born, what body they're born into, what they believe, or how they have lived their life so far.

This isn't a book written only for people who are already leaders. This book is written for leaders within global corporations, and also for someone who manages a corner store in the UK or a bodega in Manhattan with a team of people who work at the cash register. It's for managers who work on building sites and in restaurants or transportation as much as it is for people who work in offices and banks.

Everyone who works or lives anywhere in this world deserves to have great leadership in their lives, and you deserve to be a leader worth following, too.

Each chapter shares tools, perspectives, and resources that I have gathered after years of research in the field, models drawn from the world of psychology and human potential, thousands of hours of coaching leaders around the world, and my own personal practice as someone who has worked hard to be a leader. Chapter by chapter this book will build a roadmap for you, and it will help you become a leader who is worth following.

There are literally thousands of books, a multitude of TED Talks, and an ocean of training programs offering a blueprint for the right way to lead. The only possible conclusion you can draw from the diversity of advice is that no one really knows, and there is no magic potion. In the words of someone I once had the honor of mentoring, "DDS, we're all just basically winging it." Quite.

I recognize the irony here that I am now writing a book about leadership, but actually I am *not* telling you how to be a great leader. The question you should ask yourself is not, "How do I be a great leader?" but, "How do I be a decent human—a human who is worth following?" Because if leadership is defined only by followership, when you are a human worth following, you will be a leader.

My hope is this book helps you develop your own style of leadership—an approach that entices and encourages followership.

PART I

THE MAJOR FRAMES

Becoming a leader worth following requires three ingredients: self-awareness, self-acceptance, and self-development, in that order. Self-awareness precedes self-acceptance, self-acceptance is necessary for self-development, and self-development is the doorway to becoming that leader worth following.

The start of the journey is to become increasingly self-aware. Once you are aware of all your gifts and all your growing edges, the work of acceptance begins. Some people have a hard time accepting that they have gifts, and so they will downplay those gifts. Other people have a hard time accepting their growing edges, so they will deny or ignore them. But denying, ignoring, or downplaying our gifts and growing edges shows that we're missing self-acceptance, which therefore means we won't be able to develop ourselves—and that will get in our way of becoming a leader worth following.

This book isn't about changing you; it's about helping you become even more *you*, with increasing amounts of skill and flexibility.

The question you may now have is, "How do I become increasingly self-aware?"

You do so by having trusted advisors, coaches, or a partner or friend who will hold up the mirror and show you things that you don't see. You can also use certain models and tools to reflect on what that means to you and where you are in relation to these models.

That's where these Major Frames come in. The Major Frames are tools that, over the last couple of decades of working with leaders on their development and growth, I have found to be particularly useful in problem-solving, shifting your thinking, and promoting self-awareness.

I discovered some of these frames in my travels and professional experiences. Some I learned as I was studying psychology, while others I learned as I was studying coaching. Some of them I learned as I was studying neuro linguistic programming (NLP).[6]

---

6 Neuro linguistic programming (NLP) was founded in the 1970s by Richard Bandler (a mathematician, computer programmer, and therapist) and John Grinder (a world-renowned linguist). Bandler and Grinder were heavily influenced by the Human Potential Movement and by Gregory Bateson (anthropologist, social scientist, linguist, and systems thinker), Fritz and Laura Perls (the founders of Gestalt psychotherapy), Virginia Satir (family therapist), and Milton Erickson (psychiatrist, family therapist, and founding president of the American Society for Clinical Hypnosis). While NLPt certainly developed from this body of work, NLPt practitioners trace the roots of the field even further back to Alfred Korzybski's notion that "the map is not the territory," to George Kelly's *The Psychology of Personal Constructs*, and to the work of George A. Miller, the cognitive scientist.

I call them *frames* because when you place them around a situation or challenge you are facing, they enable you to look at that same situation with new eyes or with a different perspective. I have included them here to encourage you to stop and think, to realize what you think might not be true, that your perceptions are only that—perceptions. There are things that you are likely doing, consciously and unconsciously, that support or detract from your ability to engender followership. Reflect upon where you currently are, using these frames and the questions for self-reflection immediately following each frame (they are the same for each chapter).

The wonderful thing about the frames is that when I share them with a leader, they may not resonate with that person in that moment, but 100 percent of the time, at some point in that person's self-improvement journey, that Major Frame has come in handy.

You might read them and think, "Okay, this doesn't impact me right now," but they stick with you and they burrow their way back to the front of your brain at the right time.[7] They will come back and will be useful at

---

7   I guess they are the leadership equivalent of a meme!

some point, and now you'll have them in your pocket when that time arrives.

Each frame has been gathered from the worlds of psychology, human potential, and business, and I have credited the authors and original sources where known. We are forever indebted to their genius.

CHAPTER 1

THE FACE MAP

This frame lets us know how two people can be at the exact same event but walk away with two completely different experiences.

Many years ago, my husband, Davis, and I went to a Kylie Minogue concert in Manchester, in the UK. We went to dinner with our friends, had a few drinks, and then went to the concert. At the concert, we sat side by side, and we listened to the same songs. We watched the same dancing, and we saw the same costume changes. We cried at the same time and laughed at the same time. We sang the lyrics together at the same time.

We left the venue together, went back to our hotel room

(still together), and slept in the same bed. Then we got up the next day and met up with our friends...and somehow related two *completely different* stories about the concert, as if we had been in two completely different places, doing entirely unrelated things. If we hadn't both mentioned the name Kylie Minogue, you'd have no idea we were even attempting to describe the same event.

Despite having been literally *side by side* that entire night, we recounted the song order differently and disagreed about whether or not she sang one particular song. I was waxing lyrical about when she sang "The Loco-Motion" and Davis said, "She didn't sing 'The Loco-Motion' last night."

"What concert were you at?" I asked. "Because I was there when she sang 'The Loco-Motion,' and it was amazing."

"Okay," Davis replied, "but she didn't sing 'The Loco-Motion.'"

WHAT IS THE FACE MAP?

As you can see from the example of our dueling Kylie Minogue concert experiences, the map of reality that we carry around inside our heads is not an exact representation of the territory outside our heads.[8] And yet, that map we have inside our heads is incredibly important to us. It is our map of reality.

But that's the thing about it: it is only our map. It is only our reality. It is not fact; it is our fact. It is not truth; it is our truth.

Again, the Face Map lets us know how two people can be at the exact same event but can walk away with two completely different experiences.

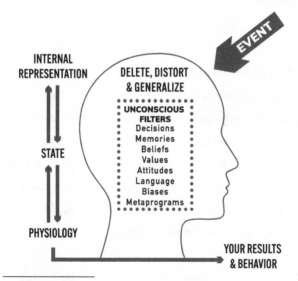

---

8   *One* of us has to be wrong about whether or not she sang "The Loco-Motion!" (I know who my vote is for.)

The Face Map, or Communication Model as it is also known, was first published in Dr. Tad James and Dr. Wyatt Woodsmall's 1998 book, *Time Line Therapy and the Basis of Personality* and has since been used by NLP practitioners around the world. It presents a way of understanding how human beings code, store, and give meaning to their experience and construct their reality.

An explanation of this model always starts with Mihaly Csikszentmihalyi who, in his 1990 book, *Flow: The Psychology of Optimal Experience*, estimated that every second our brain receives more than two million bits of information through our five senses.

Of course, without either imploding or exploding, we cannot pay attention to that much information, so we unconsciously deploy three universal and unconscious processes known as *deletion*, *distortion*, and *generalization* to filter this information down to what cognitive scientist George A. Miller called the "magic number seven, plus or minus two chunks," which he claimed to be the cognitive processing capacity of a human being.

These three universal processes are both enabling and limiting in their nature.

Deletion is the process of selectively paying attention to some aspects of our experience and not others. We use deletion to block out background noise at a social gathering when we are trying to have an intimate conversation. It is through the exact same process that someone doesn't fully take in the meaning behind acknowledgment or recognition at work. For example, you are thanked by your manager for delivering a piece of work and respond with, "I was just doing my job."

Distortion is the process of taking in aspects of our sensory experience and changing them to fit our model of the world so we can make sense of them. The process of distortion is the basis of our imagination. If you have children at home (or if you can remember being a child) you will know how easy it is for them to turn "bump in the night" into "monsters under the bed." We can use the process of distortion in an enabling way when we move house and imagine on which wall our TV is going to be hung, or where our couch is going to go. We also use it when we create, innovate, or brainstorm at work. But this process can also be deployed in a limiting way—for example, when we turn someone's kind gestures toward us into ulterior motives.

Generalization is the process of taking one, two, or

more experiences and drawing global conclusions. Without generalization, we wouldn't be able to learn. It is through this process that we can chunk together discrete actions into one capability. For example, do you remember what it was like learning to drive? It starts with a series of tasks and steps like mirror, signal, maneuver and, if you drive a car with a manual transmission, the challenge of managing the accelerator and clutch. But soon enough, these individual steps become one, and no doubt there are times when you drive from A to B without paying too much attention to what has been happening with your feet and your hands because your conscious attention has been focused on the traffic and what's happening on the road. This application of generalization is crucial to existence.

Generalization is also used in the creation of our beliefs, which can be enabling or limiting. For example, when a child touches the oven door when there is a pie being baked, they will likely burn their fingers. From this one experience, they may generalize a belief not to touch the oven door for fear of harming themselves. But this is the same process through which little girls learn to be prim, pretty, and proper, and little boys learn it is not okay to cry. It doesn't take a genius to work out what happens to the adult who as a child believed these things to be true.

UNCONSCIOUS FILTERS

We use a range of unconscious filters to direct the manner in which we delete, distort, and generalize. These filters are our decisions, memories, beliefs, values, attitudes, language, biases, and metaprograms, which I will describe here:

1. **Decisions.** The decisions we've made, and therefore the beliefs we've created in the past impact the way we perceive events in the now through a process known as Confirmation Bias.

2. **Memories.** We use our experience of the past to decide how we feel about the present and to predict the way future events will unfold.

3. **Beliefs.** The emotionally held generalizations we make about what is true and what is not true about ourselves and our world.

4. **Values.** The criteria we use to judge good/not good; our ethical and moral compass. Values govern all

human behavior because they are what is important to us in our lives. We will talk more about the topic of values in Chapter 6.

5. **Attitudes.** The combination of our values and beliefs about a given subject or context.

6. **Language.** A critical filter. It is the filter by which we label and give meaning to our experience and then express our experience outwardly to the world.

7. **Biases.** The judgments and assessments we make of people and situations influenced by our background, cultural environment, and personal experiences.

8. **Metaprograms.** Our most unconscious filters. They're content-free, context-related. An example would be our Myers–Briggs Type.[9] For a full explanation of metaprograms, see Shelle Rose Charvet's excellent book, *Words That Change Minds: The 14 Patterns for Mastering the Language of Influence.*

---

9   Based on the theories of psychologist Carl Jung, the Myers–Briggs Type Indicator (MBTI) is an introspective self-report questionnaire indicating differing psychological preferences in how people perceive the world and make decisions.

INTERNAL REPRESENTATION + STATE + PHYSIOLOGY = EXTERNAL BEHAVIOR

Having deleted, distorted, and generalized an event that we have experienced through our five senses, we internally re-present that event in the form of pictures, sounds, feelings, and words—we call this an Internal Representation (IR).

Our IRs are important. They form the basis of our map of the world; they are our reality. But this model also helps us see that our experience of events can never be the same as the actual event itself. Reality is, in fact, a construct.

The model shows that our IRs impact (and are impacted by) our state—a state being the sum of our emotional and mental condition at a specific moment in time.

Given that the mind and body are connected as one system, our states impact (and are impacted by) our physiology and drive our external behavior. Therefore, the quality and richness of our IRs, states, and physiology will determine the quality of our external behavior. They are all part of the same feedback and feed-forward loop. Change one, change the other.

Imagine an ongoing interaction or dialogue between two people: when listening to person A talk, person B must delete, distort, and generalize their communication "on the way in" to understand it and make meaning from it. Then person B must delete, distort, and generalize again "on the way out" to formulate and communicate their response. Person A must then delete, distort, and generalize person B's response "on the way in" to understand it and make meaning from it, and then again "on the way out" to share their response. This process of quadruple-plus deletion, distortion, and generalization is happening moment by moment in any dialogue. It should be no surprise to a leader that the thing they thought they'd agreed upon with their team doesn't get delivered in the way they thought they agreed it would be delivered.

LEADERSHIP TAKEAWAY

In our head, we all carry a map of reality and, because of the way in which we delete, distort, and generalize our experience, that map does not reflect the territory from which it came. To that end, there is always a good reason for peoples' behaviors and performance at work. Leaders who are worth following are those who respect other peoples' maps of the world.

Respecting other peoples' maps of the world is not the same as just going along with whatever they say or do, nor does it mean that you let people get away with poor performance. It does, however, mean there are always underlying reasons why someone shows up as they are and reminds you to meet your people where they are at and lead them from that place. Or as I like to say, go to their bus stop and have them get on your bus rather than having them walk to your bus stop.

Once you have gone to their bus stop and worked with them from their model of the world, it would serve you well to employ mechanisms to check your understanding of what has been communicated. One of the simplest ways to do this at the end of any dialogue, meeting, coaching, or feedback session is to simply ask the other person what their key takeaways or action points are. This will then enable clarification and correction, if required.

QUESTIONS FOR SELF-REFLECTION

After reading about this Major Frame, reflect on your answers to the following questions:

- What thoughts, feelings, and sensations did you experience as you read about this Major Frame?

- What resonated well with you? What landed?

- What resonated less well with you? What didn't land yet?

- As a result of these noticings, what have you learned?

- How does this learning impact your current leadership context?

- How does this learning help you be a leader worth following?

CHAPTER 2

WE ARE MEANING-MAKING MACHINES

As author and speaker Byron Katie, who has been described by *Time* as "a spiritual innovator for the twenty-first century," once said, "We don't hear what someone said; we imagine what they meant."

Sometimes, we even imagine what someone means when they've said nothing at all.

For example, I might text my husband, Davis, at noon on a Tuesday, but they don't text back immediately like they normally do. When I'm sitting there, holding my phone and not receiving their text, I can't *not* make interpretations about *why* I'm not receiving a response. I have to have a narrative, a story—which may or may not be true—around why they're not responding. On a good day, I might interpret Davis's silence that they are busy or they don't have their phone with them.

On a different day in this hypothetical situation, however, instead of assuming Davis is busy or they don't have their phone, I might get pissed off. I'll be angry that Davis isn't being attentive to me in some way. After a little bit, once I've stopped being angry, then I'll start to get anxious, thinking, *Well, maybe I've upset Davis. Maybe I said something before they left for work this morning, and they're so upset about it that they're intentionally not replying.*

The real reason, of course—the most obvious, logical reason—is that Davis is a school principal, and at noon on a Tuesday, Davis is probably knee-deep in eight-year-olds and probably doesn't even have their phone with them.

But here I am, on the other end of the text, making meaning out of the lack of a response. Why? Because I'm human.

MAKING MEANING OUT OF
ANYTHING—OR NOTHING

One of our most-evolved attributes is our ability to experience events and make meaning from them. We are making meaning all the time; it's something we can't *not* do. **We are meaning-making machines.**

This applies across all experiences we have. To make sense of them and accommodate these experiences into our model of the world, we have to create meaning. Meaning creates a feeling, and feelings are the glue of our memories.

Furthermore, in a weird twist of self-sabotaging dark humor, we seem to have an unnerving habit of making bad-meaning over no-meaning. We seem to find it easy to fill any gaps in our meaning with bad stuff rather than good stuff. Let me try to explain why.

As we have seen with the Face Map, we use a set of unconscious filters to construct our map of the world to make meaning out of our experience. Therefore, the meaning we make from situations—positive or negative—is directly linked to our state, physiology, and filters.

Because of this, whatever meaning we are making will inevitably show up in the way we communicate. In the next section, you will learn about how communication impacts.

YOU CANNOT NOT COMMUNICATE

In 1971, Professor Albert Mehrabian published a study under the title *Silent Messages*. In this study, he talked about the ways we make meaning from the communication we receive. He said to make sense of the communication, we pay attention to not just the words, but also to voice qualities and facial expressions. He even went as far as to apply percentages to each of these aspects of communication (7 percent for words, 38 percent for vocal qualities, and 55 percent for facial expressions). It has since become known as the 7-38-55 rule and is popular in communication seminars and trainings the world over, but it's often misquoted, misused, or misinterpreted.

Mehrabian's equations were derived from experiments dealing with communications of feelings and attitudes, and his study is only applicable where there is ambiguity in the communication. For example, when the voice qualities do not match the words (have you ever heard anyone tell you they're "fine" when really you know they're not?). In which case, tone and body language are the dominant sources of our understanding as we interpret and make sense of the communication.

When we conceive of communication as being more than just words and also including our voice qualities (i.e., tone, tempo, timbre, and volume) and our physiology (i.e., what we're doing with our hands, our posture, our eyes while we are talking...and, more importantly when we are not talking), then we can see the truth in the statement: **you cannot not communicate.**

People are always receiving information and making meaning out of what we are saying or doing and what we are not saying or doing. And the nature of the meaning we make will be directly linked to the way we feel about the other person and the quality of the relationship we have with them.

Let's explore the following examples of two different types of emails you might receive. Email #1 is from someone you know and with whom you have a good relationship and email #2 is from someone you know but with whom you have a tense relationship. Each email is a follow-up request to something they previously asked of you.

Email #1: Your meaning-making processes start the moment you hear the notification ping and see the name of the sender. You smile to yourself and think about the last time you were with this person and how good you felt after your interaction with them. You open the email immediately and read through it with a light and happy tone of voice in your head. As you read the words, you realize you had forgotten to follow up with their request and immediately ping them back with an apology. You let them know you'll attend to their request by the end of the day. You wish them a pleasant day in your sign-off and look forward to seeing them soon.

Email #2: You hear the ping as the email arrives. You look at your screen to see the name of the sender, and you might, if you are paying close enough attention, feel your heart sink slightly. "*Urgh*," you say out loud, while thinking, *What do they want now?* You don't open the email immediately; why would you? You have much better things to spend your time on. Eventually, you open the email while bracing yourself for whatever tripe is in the message. You may or may not notice the scowl on your face or the harsh tone of voice you are using in your head as you read it to yourself. By now you have turned what would otherwise have been a polite follow-up request from the sender into them nagging and harassing you. You close the email while you unruffle your feathers and get on with your work rather than attending to something this person needs from you. Eventually, when there is nothing else to do, you reopen the email and begrudgingly respond to their request, using a slightly firmer touch on your keyboard than you would normally.

LEADERSHIP TAKEAWAY

Imagine you are the sender of this email, and the manager of the person receiving it. Imagine, further, the likelihood that this is the typical response of the receiver each time they see an email land in their inbox from you. It doesn't take too much of a stretch of the imagination to see the impact this will have on productivity, work quality, performance, and the domino effect on the client, customer, or your wider team.

This Major Frame, therefore, reminds leaders about the importance of relationship building and of investing in relationships up front; of building credit in your peoples' "Bank of Goodwill."

QUESTIONS FOR SELF-REFLECTION

After reading about this Major Frame, reflect on your answers to the following questions:

- What thoughts, feelings, and sensations did you experience as you read about this Major Frame?

- What resonated well with you? What landed?

- What resonated less well with you? What didn't land yet?

- As a result of these noticings, what have you learned?

- How does this learning impact your current leadership context?

- How does this learning help you be a leader worth following?

CHAPTER 3

CAUSE>EFFECT

In 1987, when I was fifteen years old, Terry Waite, an English humanitarian, author, and envoy for the Church of England, traveled to Lebanon to try to secure the release of four hostages, including the journalist John McCarthy.

Terry was kidnapped and held captive until 1991; much of that time was spent in solitary confinement. He spent 1,763 days and 23 ¾ hours each day in chains, was allowed one visit to the bathroom per day, endured daily beatings, and was even subjected to a mock execution by his captors.

I remember the news reports that showcased his

release as if it had happened yesterday. It was a huge event of the time in the UK. I recall Terry steadily stepping down from the plane that brought him home, smiling and waving to the crowd. The words of the BBC news presenter covering his release are still, to this day, imprinted on my memory: "There he is talking as though he has just come back from a couple of weeks away. Look at his face. Would you really think he has been away for five years? Extraordinary resilience. Quite extraordinary."

In the weeks that followed, I was gripped by the ensuing news reports and talk shows. I was intrigued by how this human had endured such terrible circumstances and emerged from them with strength, presence, and an air of causality. I remember in one of those interviews, Terry talked about his experience and the ways he was denied many simple liberties like being able to go outside, to stand up, to walk around, to go to the bathroom. I recall him talking about the way his captors took away everything, his every right, except one thing—and that was his right to choose how to respond to the terrible things that were being done to him.

Years later, in a 2016 interview on *This Morning*, a popular daytime television show in the UK, Terry said of his thought process while being held captive, "You have the power to break my body, you have the power to bend my mind, but my soul is not yours to possess."

Here is a man who understood the power behind the frame of Cause>Effect; that being "at cause" is greater than being "at effect."

CAUSE   **EFFECT**

$$C > E$$

**BEING "AT CAUSE" IS GREATER
THAN BEING "AT EFFECT"**

So, what does that mean?

For every stimulus, there is a response; for every cause, there is an effect. It's an immutable law. We can think about this law in terms of an equation in which Cause is greater than Effect. And we can apply this equation to our lives and assume a position at either side of the equation.

To the right of the equation, when we are "at effect," we've given our power away. This is where we look to others as the reason for our situation, where we make excuses for not having done something, or for having done something we perhaps aren't that proud of. It's where we attribute the source of our experience to "them" or an "other"—the government, the weather, luck, and so on.

To the left of the equation, when you are "at cause," you're empowered, and you take accountability. It is from here where you take responsibility for generating who, what, and where you are at. No one can place you "at cause"; no one can bestow responsibility on you, and you cannot bestow it on anyone else.

"The traffic made me late." "This pen makes my handwriting messy." "They made me lose my cool." These are all statements of effect. Try these more causal ways of expressing the same thing. "Sorry I'm late; I didn't account for traffic when I planned my journey." "I am not used to using this type of pen and find it challenging to write in my usual style." "I realize I lost my cool for a moment. Something you said/did led me to recall an unpleasant memory."

In short, when you are "at cause," you're ready to own

life. It's where you hold yourself accountable and where you can say to yourself, "I am where I am and who I am today because of something I have done, or not done, in the past."

THE SPACE BETWEEN

Viktor Frankl, a neurologist, psychologist, Holocaust survivor, and author of *Man's Search for Meaning*, is believed by many to have once said, "Between stimulus and response there is a space. In that space is our power to choose our response. In our response lies our growth and our freedom."

While these words never actually appeared in any of Frankl's works, they resonate deeply with me, and they appear to chime with Terry Waite's experience mentioned earlier. With that said, sometimes the space between stimulus and response evades us. Sometimes it can be so infinitesimal that it doesn't feel like a gap at all, and our response to a certain stimulus can feel like an impulse that we have no choice over.

But what if you could linger in the space between cause and effect? What if you took a breath before responding? There is so much wisdom in the various sayings designed to provide perspective, such as "Count to ten," "Go for a walk around the block," or "Why don't you sleep on it?"

LEADERSHIP TAKEAWAY

Never in the history of being "at cause" has anyone moved from being "at effect" to being "at cause" by being told by someone else to be "at cause," so please be careful with how you go about using this Major Frame.

As we will discuss in Chapter 10, the leader is never not role modeling for their people—good or bad—and they will always get the performance and behavior from their team members that they deserve.

Given all of this, it behooves the leader to let demonstration be the teacher and to show their team how to be "at cause," because being "at cause" underpins the process of accountability, which is discussed more in Chapter 11.

QUESTIONS FOR SELF-REFLECTION

After reading about this Major Frame, reflect on your answers to the following questions:

- What thoughts, feelings, and sensations did you experience as you read about this Major Frame?

- What resonated well with you? What landed?

- What resonated less well with you? What didn't land yet?

- As a result of these noticings, what have you learned?

- How does this learning impact your current leadership context?

- How does this learning help you be a leader worth following?

CHAPTER 4

PERCEPTION IS PROJECTION

One day, when I was the chief learning and culture officer at an advertising agency, I was chatting with a member of my team, named Leticia. Leticia and I were talking about another colleague, Jane, and Leticia was saying how much she loved Jane and waxing lyrical about Jane's abilities and skills. At the very end, just as she finished talking, Leticia said, "I see so much of me in Jane."

Of course, Jane wasn't Leticia; Jane was her own person, and was so much more than the skills, qualities, behaviors, and associations that Leticia made about her. But

Leticia saw in Jane what she saw in herself, from an enabling perspective.

The same also applies in reverse. I worked with a head of sales, a guy named Igor, who was complaining about a client of theirs because of the way that client treated Igor's team. The client, an SVP in a big organization, was questioning and demanding and described by others as "challenging to work with."

Igor told me that he was going to an awards ceremony, and this client was going to be there. "You know what, DDS?" He told me, "I'm going to walk up to that client and I'm going to tell them straight to their face that they bloody well need to stop giving my team a hard time!"

I took a deep breath, sat back, and looked at Igor. Then I asked him, "On what level do you think *you* need to stop giving your team a hard time?"

The blood drained from his face. He looked at me and said, "F you," but he was smiling.

Igor realized that part of the problem was how annoyed he was at an unconscious level with himself for the way he sometimes behaved toward his team—but it was easier for him to make somebody else the pariah rather than himself. (As you'll see in just a moment, Perception is Projection tells us that it's easier for us to name traits and behaviors that are undesirable in other people than to own them for ourselves.)

I simply replied, "You're welcome."

TO PERCEIVE IS TO PROJECT

In psychodynamic psychology, projection is one of a set of "psychological defenses," which are a set of actions, thought patterns, and behaviors that humans use to separate themselves from unwanted feelings, such as guilt, shame, or anxiety, and threats to our well-being.

Projection is the psychological process of attributing our own unacknowledged, unacceptable, or unwanted thoughts and emotions onto another person. Projection reduces anxiety by allowing the expression of the undesirable impulses or desires without us having to become consciously aware of them.

This can be a complicated and uncomfortable Major Frame to grasp, so I like to describe three "levels" to understanding it, each one becoming progressively more complex. Let's take a closer look at each.

LEVEL I: PERCEPTION, NOT FACT

Given the wisdom of the Face Map explained in Chapter 1, this frame reminds you that your perception of external events is a reflection of your own map of the world and is a deleted, distorted, and generalized version of the actual event. It can never be a true facsimile of the event itself. Reality is a construct.

When a judgment about a person, situation, or event comes into consciousness, it is important to remember that this judgment is not a fact; it is just your perception. Further, this frame reminds us to check ourselves and the source or root cause of this perception before we project it onto that person, situation, or event.

LEVEL II: THE PERSONA AND THE SHADOW

Back in the day, the Swiss psychologist Carl Jung, in his conception of the psyche, unconscious mind, and personality, put forward the idea of two psychic entities that play a major role in the way we perceive and show up in the world. He called these entities the Persona and the Shadow.

We can think of the Persona as our very own shop window into which we place the aspects of our personality and character that we want the world to see. The Shadow is the opposite of this. It's like the stockroom in the back where we have placed unused, unloved, or disowned aspects of our personality and character.

The contents of our Shadow have an annoying (or useful, depending from which perspective you look at this) habit of reminding us that they exist through a process known as Shadow Projection. Through Shadow Projection, we attribute to others that which we have repressed in ourselves in the form of judgments, aspersions, and unkind thoughts.

A simple way to think about this is when you are pointing the finger at someone else, there are always three fingers pointing back at yourself. Your perception of them is a projection of something disowned, disallowed, unresolved, or unprocessed in yourself.

LEVEL III: THERE'S NOBODY ELSE OUT THERE, ONLY YOU

When we can accept the concept of Shadow Projection, we can also begin to understand that judgments and perceptions made about self or others are—on some level—judgments and perceptions about self.

My perception of you is a reflection of me; my reaction to you is an awareness of me.

LEADERSHIP TAKEAWAY

Over the past couple of decades of working with leaders, I have found there to be a direct correlation between their ability to assume positive intent and give people the benefit of the doubt (the importance of which I explore in Chapter 12), and the extent to which they are unaware of their own projections.

Assuming positive intent and giving others the benefit of the doubt are important ingredients of empathy (again, explored more in Chapter 12). Without empathy, our social relationships at work are negatively impacted, which can get in the way of performance, collaboration, and work quality.

Perception Is Projection is a useful frame in the context of leadership as a behavior not a title, simply because it reminds us to take a minute before casting aspersions and ask ourselves a simple question: "In what way is this judgment I am making of them a disowned or disallowed aspect of me?"

QUESTIONS FOR SELF-REFLECTION

After reading about this Major Frame, reflect on your answers to the following questions:

- What thoughts, feelings, and sensations did you experience as you read about this Major Frame?

- What resonated well with you? What landed?

- What resonated less well with you? What didn't land yet?

- As a result of these noticings, what have you learned?

- How does this learning impact your current leadership context?

- How does this learning help you be a leader worth following?

CHAPTER 5

THE DRAMA TRIANGLE

A long, long time ago, when I was not the person I am today, I would often spot people in need. Instead of tapping into my own vulnerability (and perhaps through a process of ESP), I would see the vulnerability in those other people and want to swoop in to save the day. I'd want to fix things for them and make things better. I'd want to take them under my wing.

In fact, a person named Gareth worked on my team, and I wanted to take him under my wing. I wanted to give him a leg up, take away his problems, and make things easy for him. Really, I wanted to rescue him.

When he accepted my rescuing tendencies, it was great. I was happy, and I felt like I was doing the job I was supposed to do—that I was a good manager. But there were times when he resisted my approaches to rescue, fix, and shield him from harm. Then I'd get really annoyed. I'd have feelings of anger, frustration, or exasperation toward him. So then I would start pointing out his weaknesses or perhaps being a bit tougher on him than the situation warranted. I used those persecuting behaviors until he became the victim, so I could then rescue him again.

We played that game for many years, until we both learned about the Drama Triangle, at which point we realized there was a dysfunctional pattern in our relationship, and we were able to address it. It was only then that I could see that what I was doing wasn't rescuing him. I was actually holding him back from his own development and growth.

THE BEGINNINGS OF THE DRAMA TRIANGLE

In the late 1950s, Eric Berne, a Canadian psychiatrist, walked away from his training in psychoanalysis, studied under Erik Erikson, and developed a body of work called Transactional Analysis, or TA as it is often referred to.

TA is a social psychology that outlines how we have developed and how we relate and communicate with others. It is underpinned by the philosophy that: (a) people can and do develop and change across their life span, and (b) that we all have a right to be in the world and be accepted.

While TA might not be as mainstream as other psychological theories, aspects of the work are extremely well known. For example, the Parent-Adult-Child model originates from Berne's work, and his 1964 book, *Games People Play: The Psychology of Human Relationships*, has sold more than five million copies since its publication.

In 1968, Stephen B. Karpman, MD, who studied under Berne, published an essay entitled "Fairy Tales and Script Drama Analysis," in which he described the Drama Triangle.

The Drama Triangle gives us one way to understand the unconscious roles people can assume in day-to-day relationships to get our needs met. We get "hooked" into the triangle by the behavior of other people. Once hooked, we respond with a "complementary" behavior, and so the "game" begins. In some instances, this series of complementary transactions can go on indefinitely and may take the form of a lifelong friendship, marriage, or pattern of behaviors across multiple contexts.

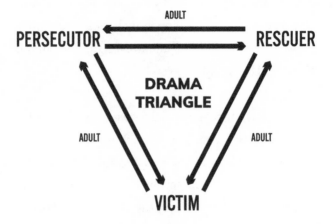

ROLES IN THE DRAMA TRIANGLE

Each of the Drama Triangle roles (Persecutor, Rescuer, Victim) is taken up as a result of a particular issue being discounted or disowned, as we saw in Chapter 4. A key point to remember is that these roles get taken up unconsciously.

The Rescuer tends not to own their own vulnerability and seeks instead to rescue those whom they see as vulnerable. One of the typical traits of a Rescuer is that they often do more than 50 percent of the work and they may offer help unasked rather than find out if and how the other person wants to be supported;

what the Rescuer agrees to do may in actual fact not be what they really want to do.

This means the Rescuer may then often end up feeling resentful, used, unappreciated, or treated unfairly in some way. The Rescuer does not take responsibility for themselves but rather takes responsibility for the perceived Victim whom they rescue. The Rescuer may end up feeling like a Victim, but sometimes may be perceived by others as being the Persecutor.

A Victim tends to feel overwhelmed by their own sense of vulnerability, inadequacy, or powerlessness. They do not take responsibility for themselves or their own power, and therefore they look for a Rescuer to take care of them. At some point, the Victim may feel let down, overwhelmed, or even persecuted by their Rescuer. When this happens, the Victim can unconsciously move to the Persecutor position and admonish their Rescuer. They may even enlist another Rescuer to persecute the previous Rescuer. All along, though, the Victim will still experience themselves internally as being the Victim.

The Persecutor might be unaware of their own power and therefore may discount it. Either way, the power used is negative and often destructive. Any person in the "game" may at any time be experienced as the Persecutor by the other people. However, their own internal perception may be that they are being persecuted and that they are the Victim.

There are, of course, instances in which the Persecutor is knowingly and maliciously persecuting the other person. When this is the case, then strictly speaking, the Persecutor is no longer playing a "game" in the TA sense of the word, as the Persecutor is operating from a place of conscious awareness.

Here is an example of how the Drama Triangle can show up:

Person A gets irritated with something that Person B does. Instead of sharing their feelings and inviting Person A into a conversation that might lead to resolution, they project those feelings onto the other person in an interaction designed to put them down (Persecutor).

Person B loses touch with a sense of their own power and takes on Person A's blame and makes the problem their own (Victim).

Person A senses all is not well with Person B and tries to make it all better by telling Person B that they are fine, that they should not worry, and that no damage has really been done at all (Rescuer).

Person B senses this switch in energy and approach from Person A and feels irritated. Instead of sharing their feelings, they project them onto Person A in such a way that puts Person A back in their box (Persecutor).

Sensing the switch in energy and approach, Person A feels bad and emotionally withdraws (Victim), which triggers Person B's Rescuer.

LEADERSHIP TAKEAWAY

Depending on the structure of your unconscious filters (as seen in the Face Map in Chapter 1), you may have a predilection for a particular Drama Triangle role.

As we already know, our beliefs shape our perceptions and, combined with our values, govern all human behavior. To that end, an examination of your beliefs about leadership might be in order and may provide some clues as to how you find yourself in the Drama Triangle more often than you would like.

For example, a leader who holds beliefs around perfectionism, delivery at any cost, or has a fear of failure may find themselves hooked into the Persecutor role. A leader who believes they must have all the answers, cannot let go of the details, or worries unduly about the stress or pressure their team is under could well end up in the Rescuer role. A leader who lacks belief in themselves, is worried about whether other people think they are up to the job, or who is plagued with "imposter syndrome" may succumb to the Victim role.

We will explore more about the impact of beliefs about self (especially self-limiting beliefs) and how these impact leadership behavior in Chapter 10.

QUESTIONS FOR SELF-REFLECTION

After reading about this Major Frame, reflect on your answers to the following questions:

- What thoughts, feelings, and sensations did you experience as you read about this Major Frame?

- What resonated well with you? What landed?

- What resonated less well with you? What didn't land yet?

- As a result of these noticings, what have you learned?

- How does this learning impact your current leadership context?

- How does this learning help you be a leader worth following?

CHAPTER 6

THE NEUROLOGICAL
LEVELS OF CHANGE

Imagine a couple who is having relationship problems. They are arguing frequently, finding it hard to communicate with each other, and are not having as much sex as either of them would like. So, they decide that a nice vacation will do them a world of good. They book a weeklong trip to Turks and Caicos where they lie happily on the beach drinking mai tais for hours, reading books, enjoying each other's company, and having deep and meaningful conversations. They even find themselves having sex every afternoon before dinner!

By the end of the vacation, they feel like a new couple

and wonder why they didn't do this sooner. Then they hop on a plane, return home, and soon thereafter the same problems return. The couple begins to feel like all hope is lost and both of them secretly consider ending the relationship because of the apparent lack of love and desire.

Their "problems" are with their behavior, but their solution was to change their context by going on vacation. Sure enough, given that all meaning is context dependent, when they changed their context, their behavior temporarily shifted, but when they returned home, the same old behavior patterns returned.

Had the couple known about Logical Levels, which you're going to see in the next section, they may have chosen, instead, to work on their shared identity or values and beliefs as a couple (which, by the way, is the approach that many couples therapists take when working with clients).

WHAT ARE THE NEUROLOGICAL LEVELS OF CHANGE?

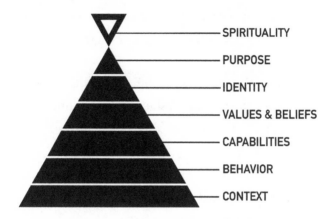

SPIRITUALITY

PURPOSE

IDENTITY

VALUES & BELIEFS

CAPABILITIES

BEHAVIOR

CONTEXT

The theory of Logical Levels was first put forward by Gregory Bateson, the anthropologist. He identified natural classifications and hierarchies in the process of communication, learning, and personal change. Robert Dilts, a developer, author, trainer, and consultant in the field of NLP since 1975, studied personally with Gregory Bateson and developed the model of Neurological Levels from his work.

The model suggests a hierarchy of levels of processes within an individual and groups. The function of each level is to synthesize, organize, and direct the function of the level below.

Here's a description of each level:

Context: This level refers to our outer world, the communities, circles, and systems in which we exist.

Behavior: What we do, say, think, and feel. Our behavior is the external manifestation of our values and beliefs and is the external expression of the self.

This model helps us to see that our behavior and our identity are different. What we do is not who we are. This is a useful distinction to make.

Capabilities: These are also known as competencies, the collection of our skills, knowledge, and behaviors into mental maps, strategies, or competencies. Organizationally, this level would include the company's systems, processes, and policies.

Values and Beliefs: Values govern all behavior. For both an individual and an organization, values are the criteria used to judge good/bad or right/wrong; they are an ethical and moral compass.

Our beliefs are emotionally held generalizations about what we see as being true about the world around us.

They are the permissions and boundaries for how the world is. We organize our perceptions according to our beliefs; as such, they might be considered as self-fulfilling prophecies. In the words of Henry Ford, "If you think you can do a thing or think you can't do a thing, you're right."

Identity: This level refers to who we are and how we think of ourselves as a person, team, or organization. This is what we are referring to when we use the words "I am," "You are," "We are," and "They are."

We are a process of actions, thoughts, feelings, behaviors, and emotions. We are made up of a collection of memories, experiences, values, beliefs, and capabilities. There is always more to someone than meets their "I."

Purpose: This is our "Why?" It's our mission, or the reason we get out of bed in the morning. As we will explore in Chapter 8, leaders who are worth following always start with "Why?"

Spirituality: This refers to the larger system of which we are a part and your connection to something bigger than ourselves.

LEADERSHIP TAKEAWAY

Changing something at a lower level may not necessarily affect anything in the upper levels; however, changing something in the upper levels would change and reorganize what's happening in the lower levels. This model is, therefore, really useful in diagnosing, analyzing, and fixing organizational development issues at either the individual, team, departmental, or organizational level because it can help us determine "where" we might be holding or maintaining a problem, and from where we need to work to address the issue systemically.

Note: the wisdom of this model tells us that the solution to an issue does not exist at the same level as the issue, but at least two levels above.

I shared one example of how this model can be useful at the beginning of the chapter, with the couple having relationship problems. Now, let's take this into the workplace.

Imagine, if you will, that there are two teams who need to work together but who spend a lot of their time blaming each other for not delivering their part, throwing turds over the fence at each other and throwing each other under the bus in separate meetings with their leader. Sound familiar? The leader of the team is at the end of their tether and, without knowledge of Logical Levels, decides to take the team on a fun afternoon out of the office and books an Escape Room, a swanky dinner afterward, and ends the evening in a karaoke bar.

Sure enough, as the day progresses and the drinks flow, the two teams get along famously, and by the end of the evening, they are professing their love for each other while singing "Greased Lightning" at the tops of their voices. This adoration and appreciation for each other lasts for a week or so, but sooner than later the problematic behaviors return, and the leader feels like giving up!

Over the years of my career, I have advised on, supported, and facilitated more "team building" exercises than I can remember, and I am a big proponent of bringing people together to break bread and build social relationships, but only when this is in addition to—and not instead of—the real work of turning a group of people into a team. So, had this leader bolstered the investment they made in the event with some interventions at the Purpose, Identity, and Values and Beliefs level, they would likely be experiencing a sustained change in the discordant behaviors of their two teams.

Note, another typical reaction to poor communication (i.e., behavior) between teams is colocation, or having the two teams sit together. Just like the "Greased Lightning" example, this affects change at the level of context, which will not lead to sustained change at any of the levels already mentioned.

QUESTIONS FOR SELF-REFLECTION

After reading about this Major Frame, reflect on your answers to the following questions:

- What thoughts, feelings, and sensations did you experience as you read about this Major Frame?

- What resonated well with you? What landed?

- What resonated less well with you? What didn't land yet?

- As a result of these noticings, what have you learned?

- How does this learning impact your current leadership context?

- How does this learning help you be a leader worth following?

CHAPTER 7

THE LEADERSHIP PIPELINE

When I was the chief learning and culture officer at the advertising agency I've spoken about previously, we had a very clear and robust approach to company culture. When the company decided to expand into Asia, my brief was to help bring that culture to the Asian markets.

But I made a cultural blunder—I tried to copy and paste what had worked in the UK and US and apply it to Asia. I didn't recognize that what was successful previously might not work as well in another setting. And it didn't. When I tried to implement certain parts of our cultural fabric in the Asian markets, it just didn't jive with employees there. That's when I realized I was trying to implement something that was not appropriate for the context, and I would have to change my recipe for success.

That blunder I made is a mistake many executives and leaders will make in their careers as they move up through the ranks, and it's something we can learn from.

One aspect of the executive coaching we provide at Soul Trained is called inflection coaching, and it is specifically geared toward people who are at an inflection point in their career. They've either taken a step up, or a step sideways, or they've taken on more responsibility in some way. This coaching is all geared around the idea that what got you here isn't going to get you there.

In general, across my work, I often see people get promoted on the strength of what they have done and who they have been, only to try to deploy their same "recipe for success" and have it fail. It failed because they didn't recognize that when they move into a new role at a new level—or in a new context—that what worked *then* might not work *now*.

WHAT DOES THE LEADERSHIP PIPELINE LOOK LIKE?

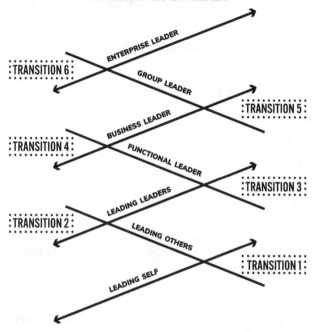

As we know, all meaning is context dependent—when the context changes, we have to make changes, too, in order to be able to adjust to that context. Those changes involve shedding some beliefs, behaviors, and patterns, and adopting new ones.

That's where the Leadership Pipeline comes in.

Stephen Drotter, Chairman of the Leadership Pipeline

Institute, argues that there are six transitions that an individual will need to successfully navigate if they wish to take a career path from an individual contributor to the CEO of an enterprise.

When I work with leaders using this model, they tend to make sense of it by referring to it as "the leadership ladder." I like to explain the basic premise of this model this way:

- There are different levels, or rungs, of leadership.

- At each rung, a leader has a different kind of leadership job.

- There is an inflection point between each rung, which, if transitioned successfully, will enhance the extent to which the leader is worth following as they continue to climb the ladder.

Drotter suggests there is no shortcut and that managing a successful transition at each inflection point is critical. While the role of the leader is very different on each level, Drotter argues that there are four common attributes that are vital to successful transition at any rung of the ladder:

- You have to learn new skills.

- You have to dial down, or let go of, skills and ways of working that had historically made you successful.

- You must make a value shift; i.e., what was important to you needs to become less important and what wasn't important needs to become important.

- You must, therefore, focus your effort and spend your time differently.

There seems to be a consistent phenomenon in the sectors I work in and with the leaders I work with, which is the apparent need to prove that you are doing the job before you get the job; that internal promotion ability seems to rely on your ability to demonstrate that you can do the job of the next rung on the ladder before you are given it.

This is one reason I find Drotter's model to have such broad appeal with leaders, the idea of the inflection point being that liminal space in which you feel as though you have outgrown your current level, but still need to demonstrate to others that you are ready to move on up.

In this next section, I share a summary of each rung of the "leadership ladder," along with the typical shifts a leader needs to make at each transition point.[10]

LEADING SELF

Bearing in mind Goffee and Jones's wisdom I mentioned earlier (and will explore in subsequent chapters), leadership is nonhierarchical; it has nothing to do with your pay grade and everything to do with how you show up in an organization. This, I believe, is the essence of the first "rung" of the leadership ladder.

Transition 1: The principal shifts that are required to successfully transition the inflection point between leading self and leading others are that of valuing managerial work. In other words, finding enjoyment in the supervision of other people and all the new behaviors said managerial work requires, as well as valuing the experience of getting stuff done through others versus valuing getting stuff done ourselves.

---

10   A full description can be found in Stephen Drotter's 2011 book, *The Leadership Pipeline*.

LEADING OTHERS

The next rung on the ladder tends, I believe, to be fraught with the tension of "doing management work" versus "doing my work." I often hear leaders at this level talking about the extra time it takes to be a manager and supervise others. They see the leadership part of their job as additional, or something that comes on top of their actual job. This is a telltale sign that they did not yet successfully transition through the first inflection point, and I would assert that until the "management work" is integrated and perceived to be *the* job, leaders will be able to climb future rungs of the ladder, but they place at risk the perception by others of being worth following or not.

Transition 2: To successfully transition through the second inflection point and toward the third rung of the ladder where they begin to lead leaders, the leader has to recognize that they are distancing themselves even further from the "doing" of their job and must further embrace the "being" side. This requires placing greater value on the various behaviors after which each of the chapters in Part II are named.

LEADING LEADERS

The conversations I tend to have with leaders at this level focus on the idea of "let go and lead." It really is a time of moving back and getting out of other peoples' way. Leaders can become bottlenecks very quickly if they don't get up and out of the day-to-day detail[11] and recognize that they are more of a conductor than they are a member of the orchestra.

Transition 3: A key skill required at this level is the ability to lead areas outside of your own expertise, meaning you must not only understand foreign work but learn how to value it. Leaders running any kind of self-limiting beliefs (SLB), which I will discuss more in Chapter 10, will find this inflection point tricky and may get stuck.

LEADING FUNCTIONS

Leaders also need to become proficient strategists, not only for their functional strategy but for blending their strategy with the overall business strategy. This means collaborating with other functional leaders, taking a

---

11   While particularly significant at rung three of the leadership ladder, the idea of getting up and out of the weeds of your comfort zone applies at every subsequent level. It can be incredibly damaging to followership if leaders don't get this right.

bigger-picture view of what success looks like, and placing increasing amounts of value on goals shared by a cross-functional team versus individual outcomes and achievements.

Transition 4: The inflection point is not simply a matter of becoming more strategic and cross-functional in your thinking. The leader must demonstrate that they are ready to lead a business by making more time for reflection and analysis and by shifting their perspective from looking at plans functionally ("Can we do it?") to looking at things from a commercial perspective ("Will we make money?" and "Is it sustainable?").

LEADING A BUSINESS

To be successful, business leaders must value, trust, accept advice, and receive feedback from all functional leaders beneath them, even if they have never experienced these functions personally. Directing and energizing support groups like HR, finance, and legal are crucial business-leader responsibilities. When the leader of the business demeans these roles, their business will deliver half-hearted results.

Transition 5: Leadership at the next level becomes

more holistic. Successfully navigating this inflection point requires leaders to show that they can cope with bigger decisions, greater risk, and increasing amounts of uncertainty and ambiguity—all skills that are essential to running a group.

A business manager values the success of his own business, whereas a group manager values the success of other peoples' businesses. To that end, an important value shift here is to move from valuing one's own success to valuing the success of others.

LEADING A GROUP

Drotter talks about four key skillsets of a group leader:

1. Evaluating capital allocation. This means deciding which strategy has the best chance of success and therefore should be funded.

2. Portfolio strategy. Being able to ask questions like: Do I have the right collection of businesses? What businesses should be added or subtracted to position us properly?

3. Succession Planning. This entails identifying

which Function Leaders are ready to become Business Leaders.

4. Assessing core capabilities. Becoming astute at assessing whether you have the right core capabilities across the group and ensuring that they are more than the sum of their parts.

Transition 6: To demonstrate readiness for the next level, leaders must continue their process of letting go of individual products, people, and customers. They must focus on the performance of the whole group and find ways to contribute and collaborate with other leaders, at the enterprise level. They must show an ability to be a long-term thinker, but at the same time have a handle on quarter-by-quarter performance that is in tune with their long-term strategy.

LEADING AN ENTERPRISE

Successful leadership of an enterprise tends to rest, Drotter says, on three or four high-leverage decisions annually, and Enterprise Leaders must set and focus on these three or four mission-critical priorities. Enterprise Leaders must also assemble a team of high-achieving reports knowing that some of them want the job that the Enterprise Leader currently occupies, but still picking them for the team despite this knowledge. They must also demonstrate an ability to manage shareholders, the stock market, industry bodies, and so on.

LEADERSHIP TAKEAWAY

Your growth as a leader is dependent on making transitions from one level of leadership to another, with each level demanding new skills, outlooks, and values. As you are readying yourself to take a next step, it will behoove you to consciously review your recipe for success so far and create a new one. Simply put, what got you here won't get you there.

QUESTIONS FOR SELF-REFLECTION

After reading about this Major Frame, reflect on your answers to the following questions:

- What thoughts, feelings, and sensations did you experience as you read about this Major Frame?

- What resonated well with you? What landed?

- What resonated less well with you? What didn't land yet?

- As a result of these noticings, what have you learned?

- How does this learning impact your current leadership context?

- How does this learning help you be a leader worth following?

THE SIX PRINCIPLES OF HUMAN LEADERSHIP

In the introduction, I shared with you a section that was titled after I was inspired by someone called Chris Becker in one of my leadership growth learning experiences, when he said, "You know, I've realized, DDS, that you can't choose your manager, but you do choose your leader."

So how do people choose their leader?

Over the twenty-five years of my work, study, and research in this space, I have found that there are some common principles that leaders who are worth following all share.

Those are the Six Principles of Human Leadership, which we will explore here in Part II. Each of the upcoming chapters covers one of these principles:

I. **Leaders who are worth following start with "Why?"** Leaders who are worth following will invest effort and energy into articulating a clear and compelling "Why?" for their team. It's an important task because, as Simon Sinek tells us, "People don't buy *what* you do, they buy *why* you do it." When we know why, we can be unified, we can make smarter decisions, and we can navigate a way forward with greater ease.

2. **Leaders who are worth following create the conditions for their people to be successful.** In creating the conditions for their people to be successful, leaders who are worth following use inclusive behaviors to center the voices of historically excluded communities to create a climate of belonging. They also demonstrate that they operate through "supporting lines" versus reporting lines because they understand that it is their job to make their people look good, and not the other way around—that their people don't work *for* them, but *with* them.

3. **Leaders who are worth following are worth copying.** Behavior is contagious, which means the culture of any team or organization will be shaped by the worst behavior you are willing to tolerate in a leader. The leaders who are worth following make sure their behavior is worth copying.

4. **Leaders who are worth following don't walk by.** Leaders who are worth following hold themselves and others accountable, and they demonstrate that accountability is a verb, and not just a noun. They focus on performance. They don't walk by— if something needs doing, fixing, or changing,

they take care of it. Or they bring the right people together to do it, fix it, or change it.

5. **Leaders who are worth following bring their people with them.** Everybody wants to know they are cared for and their development is important. Leaders who adopt a coaching style to their management practice, who lead with empathy, and who give their people the benefit of the doubt will engender followership, because this will show how much they care about their people, their work, and their careers.

6. **Leaders who are worth following learn from what worked and what didn't.** The leaders most worth following are the ones who recognize when they need help and aren't afraid to ask for it. They're also attuned to the times when they get it wrong, and when they do, they always say sorry—and when the shoe is on the other foot, they always assume positive intent. They are open to feedback, and they listen carefully when they receive it. Doing so means they are better placed to offer feedback when necessary. Learners like to learn from learners.

I implemented this set of principles at an organization of three thousand people with twenty-one offices around the world, where I was the chief learning and culture officer. While these principles were in use at that organization, it reported the highest levels of employee engagement it had ever recorded, as well as the lowest levels of attrition it had ever recorded. When used correctly in an organizational infrastructure, these principles have created real positive meaning and real positive impact at a global scale.

I know from the thousands upon thousands of hours I have worked individually with executives on their self-improvement in becoming a leader worth following, and from the thousands upon thousands of hours I've spent in workshops with leaders of all levels from entry-level management through to CEOs who run global enterprises, that these principles have created positive shifts in terms of the sentiment these leaders receive from the people they lead.

The goal of Part II is to describe these principles while also providing quick tools and other resources that a manager like you could use at a behavioral skill level to operationalize the principles of human leadership and thereby become a person who is worth following.

I also reached out to my network and asked people to share their personal stories about how each of these principles has showed up in—or has been missing from—their careers. At the end of each chapter, different people from different organizations around the world will describe, in their own words, their experience with leadership and how these principles appeared or did not appear for them.

CHAPTER 8

LEADERS WHO ARE WORTH FOLLOWING... START WITH "WHY?"

A group of twenty employees working at the advertising agency I've talked about in other chapters all decided to go on vacation together, and every year they would go on a ski trip in Europe. They organized the trip among themselves, which I think tells us something about the culture of that company.

One year they came back from the ski trip and told me they had made up a drinking game around the leadership principles. While I'm not encouraging drinking games, I do want to point to the fact that a group of employees became friends; they self-organized a vacation together; and on that vacation, they chose to talk about their company culture and leadership principles. That to me is a win.

How many of your employees are thinking about your company when they're on vacation, let alone discussing leadership principles? Before considering that, how many of your employees would voluntarily vacation with their coworkers? And how many then go on to become not just a group of people who work together but a true *team*?

BECOMING A TEAM

This may sound obvious, but you can't just throw a group of people together and expect them to become a team.

Most managers are managing more than one person, and the common label for that is to group those people together and call them a team. But not every group of people is worthy of the name "team." A team exhibits certain behaviors, which other authors have written tons about, so I'm not going to go into that here. I have provided just two sources that I would personally recommend, and they appear in the next section.[12]

What I do want to talk about, though, is that one of the most overlooked aspects of creating a team is ensuring there is role clarity, role acceptance, and goal clarity.

Role clarity means becoming crystal clear around roles. Who is accountable for what? Role acceptance is then ensuring that everyone accepts their own role in that group of people, and they also accept everybody else's role so they can continue to swim in their own lane while trusting that everybody else is swimming in their lane. Teams then need goal clarity, which is understanding what each individual is being measured on. What will success look like for each individual, and how will it look as a team? The group of people become a team when there is role clarity and role acceptance, but most importantly, when they have a shared perspective on what success looks like. If the experience of one person on the team is not one of

---

12 The Performance Room from PlanetK2 has a wealth of information about building high-performance teams and it's free to sign up: https://www.theperformanceroom.co.uk/ In 1965, Bricer Tuckman published a theory known as "Tuckman's stages of group development," which can be accessed easily from various online sources.

success, that means the entire team feels the experience is not successful.

It's only when you have that crystal clarity on roles, the certainty around role acceptance, and the individual and collective goal clarity that you can begin to really think of yourself not as a group but as a *team*.

FINDING YOUR WHY

From there, leaders who are worth following will invest effort and energy into articulating a clear and compelling Why for their team. It's an important task because, as Simon Sinek tells us, "People don't buy *what* you do, they buy *why* you do it."

When we know Why, we can be unified, we can make smarter decisions, and we can navigate a way forward with greater ease.

The answer to the question "Why?" taps into our motivation and is the fuel to our personal engine. Herman Cain[13] is once known to have said, "Nobody motivates

---

13 Herman Cain was an American businessman and Tea Party movement activist within the Republican Party.

today's workers. If it doesn't come from within, it doesn't come at all."

Articulating a Why means thinking through and spelling out a shared purpose and direction. It answers the questions:

- Why does my team exist?

- To what bigger-picture goal do we contribute?

- What business imperatives wouldn't happen if my team didn't exist?

- What is missing in the world that means my team must exist?

The gold standard of creating a Why is for the leader of a team to perform some self-reflection.

When you're asking yourself these questions, be mindful of the "motherhood and apple pie effect." Make sure you're not articulating something that is middle of the road, that everyone can say they like, and that could apply to anyone, anywhere. You're trying to avoid creating one of those god-awful motivational posters depicting a kitten "hanging in there," because that will result in eye rolls and disengagement.

What you're looking for is a statement that has the four qualities of a good Why: brevity, consistency, specificity, and emotionality.

BREVITY

We know from the Face Map, which is one of the Major Frames in Part I, that the cognitive processing capacity of a human being is "seven, plus or minus two chunks" of information. So, from a brevity point of view, you want your Why statement to be no longer than nine words (twelve at a push if you ignore the prepositions, but I always say go for nine). In fact, it's even better if it's six—and if that's better, what's best of all is if you can say it in one word. But keep it to a maximum of nine words, because you want people to be able to recall your Why statement.

The idea behind your Why is that you are articulating the purpose or the mission of the team. And so, everyone needs to be able to connect what they do on a day-to-day basis with why they're doing it. If you can't remember the Why, you're not going to be able to make that connection.

CONSISTENCY

The next aspect of a good Why is there has to be consistency. It doesn't have to be possible, but it should be plausible. The Why doesn't have to be true, but it *could* be true.

The consistency piece asks, "Is there enough overlap between my lived experience of being on this team and what the Why statement says? Is there consistency between the words and my experience?" Whatever is articulated has got to be close enough to the day-to-day experience while still also being aspirational, inspirational, and exciting.

SPECIFICITY

Specificity means that your Why statement must be based upon a decent amount of reflection on what the work of the team is.

When JFK went to NASA, he spoke to the janitor and asked, "What do you do here?"

The janitor, who was mopping floors at the time, looked at the president and said, "I'm sending people to the moon."

That janitor understood the assignment. They understood that they had a part in taking Apollo 13 to the moon. And they were connecting the cleanliness, the sanitation, and the presentation of the hallways of NASA and seeing that it was mission critical.

Specificity is that important in terms of there's got to be some connection related to the context.

EMOTIONALITY

Finally, your Why statement must elicit emotion. If it doesn't give you goose bumps, make your heart beat a little bit faster, or raise a smile—or worse, if you read it and go, "Meh"—it's not good enough.

The idea behind this Why statement is to give an injection of motivation. It's going to bring joy, interest, and engagement into the team. It must be something that somebody would feel good telling their friends about when they're hanging out together or sharing around the table when they go home for the holidays. When you share this Why statement, it has to generate positive feelings.

LEVEL UP YOUR WHY

The gold standard for developing a Why statement is when the manager goes away and develops it themselves through a process of self-reflection or workshopping with a coach, considering the answers to the questions I posed earlier in the chapter. The platinum standard is when that leader workshops those questions with their team so that the people on the team have some ownership of this Why. It belongs to them.

Ownership makes a huge difference as to the extent to which this will be brought to life. In an ideal world, everybody makes the mission of the team their personal mission every day. So when you get up, you are putting people on the moon and that's your mission today. Everything you do throughout the day points back to that mission in some way.

You, as the leader, will have a Why. Your team has a Why. Your department has a Why, and your company has a Why. To get all four of those to level up really takes reflection.

To what greater goal am I contributing? That's the mission of the company.

When I was the chief learning and culture officer for a global advertising agency, one of the things I always said to people was, "We will never put our mission, vision, or values on the wall." Because as soon as they go on the wall, they become a marketing campaign. And when it becomes a marketing campaign, you've lost the plot because you're trying to sell an experience to people.[14]

When we're putting stuff on the walls—or on mouse mats, screen savers, or backpacks—we become desensitized to it. We look at them all the time, so we stop actually seeing them.

What you want is for people's experiences to match the words that are written, so they feel connected and consistent with their experience. These Why statements are messages of intent and purpose designed to drive motivation and engagement. They are designed to proactively manage discretionary effort so people feel excited and engaged to come to work, to bring their best selves.

---

14 Avoid, at all costs, the reproduction of those late-nineties motivational posters with pictures of eagles soaring above mountains or dolphins leaping through rainbows above some awful platitude.

Establishing an overall Why for the team is a great driver for motivation because it can bring meaning and purpose to someone's work. Hard work without a Why can be experienced as stress and overwhelm, whereas hard work *with* a Why is often experienced as exciting. So, once you have established an overall Why for the team, the next step is to think about facilitating motivation at the individual level.

PROACTIVELY MANAGING DISCRETIONARY EFFORT

Let's consider for a moment the concept of **"supporting lines" over "reporting lines."** In this context it becomes the number one job of a manager to create the conditions for their people to be successful (a concept we'll explore more in the next chapter); it is the manager's role to make their team look good, not the other way around. These concepts sit at the core of Soul Trained's leadership growth learning experiences and workshops and are a part of the how-to of bringing to life our principle that **"leadership is a behavior, not a title."**

One of the ways in which we help leaders to think through this is by asking them how they would approach leading their people if those people were volunteering their time. In asking this question, leaders are forced to consider how they would approach managing their people if they weren't being compensated for their efforts with a salary or if they were turning up to work and giving their time out of the goodness of their heart.

While it's clearly a hypothetical question, it always creates a shift in the conversation and in the leader's outlook. Here's why.

It's true—at least in this economy—that if we want to get paid, we have to put in the hours; that we show up and we deliver the goods. What is not mandated is the way we put in the hours, the extent we will go the extra mile, and the frequency at which we will go above and beyond. All of that is discretionary (and therefore voluntary).

Picture these two scenarios for a moment:

- **Scenario #1:** You wake up late because your alarm didn't go off. You step out of bed only to find your bare foot lands in a "gift" the dog left you in the middle of the night. You stumble to the shower to find there is no hot water. After your cold shower, you realize there is no oat milk (we're in California, okay?) in the empty carton that the person you live with left in there, which means you can't eat your cereal and you have to drink your coffee black. You go to get dressed but can't find any matching socks, your hair won't do what it is supposed to do, and your generous-gifting dog has left you an additional present by chewing the toes off your shoes. By the time you make it to your desk (at home or in the office), it feels like you have already had a full day and you are far from ready to start another one. You're at work in body, but your heart and soul are still under the covers.

- **Scenario #2:** You wake up one minute before your alarm and just at the perfect moment when the happiest of dreams you were having comes to a successful conclusion. You get out of bed and take a shower of the perfect temperature. You step out of the shower to find the person you live with has placed a cup of coffee just the way you like it next to the sink with a little note to say that breakfast is ready. Having eaten the most exquisite avocado toast with a soft poached egg, microgreens, red pepper flakes, and toasted black sesame seeds (I told you we were in California), you get dressed in your power outfit (you know the one). When you check yourself in the mirror, you find yourself smiling at what is being reflected back at you. With Dolly Parton's "9 to 5" playing in your head, you are literally full of the joys of spring and are excited to get stuck into the day ahead at work.

Neither of these scenarios requires too much of a stretch of the imagination. Equally it doesn't take a genius to work out how each scenario might impact the extent to which we apply our discretionary effort.

Of course, the happenings in each of these scenarios are not influenced by a manager, but there are a number of conditions at work that the manager does directly influence. Here are just a few, which are taken from Marcus Buckingham and Curt Coffman's 1999 book, *First, Break All the Rules*, which is a result of observations based on eighty thousand interviews with managers as conducted by the Gallup organization in the last twenty-five years:[15]

---

15 And was named one of the twenty-five most influential business books of all time.

- Providing role clarity and goal clarity so that your people know what is expected of them.

- Ensuring they have the materials and equipment they need to do their work correctly.

- Regularly finding ways for them to play to their strengths and do what they do best.

- Offering praise or recognition for good work; saying "thank you."

- Demonstrating genuine care for them as a human being.

- Encouraging them to develop and grow.

Buckingham and Coffman's research showed that these six factors are highly influential over four key business metrics—profitability, productivity, client satisfaction, and employee satisfaction and retention.

I believe they are the most important inputs and ingredients in proactively managing discretionary effort, in ensuring that your people will go above and beyond because they want to and not because they have to.

Imagine, for a moment, the flip side of proactively managing discretionary effort—how much time do you think is lost by team members who are demoralized because they are unclear, not cared for, unthanked, or unheard? Without the right conditions to be successful, you're likely to see spikes in attrition and harbor team members who could be vicariously passing on their demotivation across the team.

Proactively managing discretionary effort could well be the secret weapon of the most successful businesses. You owe it to yourself, your team, and your business to do it.

EXAMPLES OF THE IMPORTANCE OF STARTING WITH WHY

At the end of each chapter (and at the beginning of some chapters as well) here in Part II, I'd like to include some real-life examples of the importance of the Six Principles of Human Leadership. These stories, opinions, and pieces of advice come from people in my network and are told using their own words.

From AS: Setting out the Why is the first thing I do. It gives everyone the needed focus and clarity to succeed. However, I have had leaders who have not set out the Why or clear intentions, and it's almost impossible to measure your success when this happens. You feel like you're always chasing something but never clear what that something is. It results in frustrations and lack of satisfaction at work. My advice: ensure you're setting everyone up for success with clarity and focus. Your Why should be strong and inspirational.

From NS: I've encountered two types of "Why-ers" in my career: those who seek to create a Why because it is for the betterment of everyone, and those who seek to engender a Why "collectively" around their own personal mission—and more often than not for their own personal gains and ego. The differences are on a sliding scale between stark and utterly ridiculous.

There are those who want to genuinely know me and who I am as a person so they can seek a harmonious place in which they can engage me and my talents in the Why. And those who think that engagement in the Why is as simple as asking me what football team I support (when I hated PE) or how my wife is, when I am the G of an LGBTQ+ family.

What impact did these two types of Why-ers have? I invested my energy into one and not the other. I simply disengaged, voted with my feet, and sought out better elsewhere.

From K: I sometimes feel as though I have not clearly articulated my company's Why to my team or myself. The result is a period of meaningless action and no progress. I often feel like I'm busy but I don't feel like I'm moving toward my goal. It isn't until I stop and recognize the Why, rearticulate, and share it with my team, that we start finding focus again.

From JW: My current boss decided to put a "sales push" initiative into place, and the reasons were to get better sales results and to start the chase to get better results earlier. The problem was the Why given was "we aren't winning enough jobs and we need more time to prepare"— but this was neither the problem nor the solution and just allowed credit to be taken by those not involved.

When a Why is given, it is important that it makes sense to those affected by it, but also that it has a positive effect on their role or a clear understanding of why, such as additional reporting for regulatory reasons. The impact of the sales push was nothing, and it has since been abandoned.

As you can see, starting with Why is an incredibly powerful foundation for becoming a leader worth following. However, it is only the first step. The next principle builds upon this strong base. Chapter 9 shows how leaders who are worth following create the conditions for their people to be successful.

CHAPTER 9

LEADERS WHO ARE WORTH FOLLOWING CREATE THE CONDITIONS FOR THEIR PEOPLE TO BE SUCCESSFUL

CD, with an example of getting this principle wrong: I once worked with the wildest, most toxic boss. I have never felt so emotionally unsafe in my life. Everyone who interacted with him at work was terrified of him. As a CEO, he created a culture of fear, where everyone was worried about retaliation if they pushed back on him. It was so bad that his COO (who became a friend of mine) would go to dinner with me and talk about how emotionally unstable he was. Truly terrifying.

Eventually I ended up quitting the job. It had gotten so bad that whenever I heard my Slack notification chime, I started having a physical response to the anxiety! He was definitely an example of a leader who did not create the right conditions.

And NS, with an example of getting it right: Back in 2019, when I joined my current organization. I had come from a company with a great equality policy, on paper, yet one that didn't really want me to be my true self. Three months into my new role, with a new brand—one of whose values is Be Yourself—I had a very open-hearted conversation with my now-manager. We talked about the version of myself I had been in my old role—this distilled, homogenized version of myself that I thought was better for my career and future. My new manager looked me straight in the eye and said, "I don't want that version of you. I want the whole of you. I give you permission here to be 100 percent yourself."

For the first time I felt like I had a manager who wanted me to be me, and for him to then "get" that me in the process.

I now lead with this at the very core of how I manage, who I recruit, and how I coach. I manage with individualization at heart, I recruit those who add, and I coach from the heart with the same respect I was shown. And it feels great!

CREATE CONDITIONS FOR SUCCESS—FOR EVERYONE

In creating the conditions for their people to be successful, leaders who are worth following use inclusive behaviors to center the voices of historically excluded communities in order to create a climate of belonging. They also demonstrate that they operate through supporting lines versus reporting lines because they understand it is their job to make their people look good, and not the other way around—that their people don't work *for* them, but *with* them.

In Chapter 8, I shared six conditions laid out by Buckingham and Coffman in their 1999 book, *First, Break All the Rules*. Their research showed that these conditions will drive four key business outcomes: employee engagement and retention, client satisfaction, employee productivity, and profitability. While important, these conditions are not the only conditions that will drive success for their team members.

In this chapter, I will discuss change management and the crucial role of the leader in supporting their team members through change and transition, as well as some coaching techniques so that team members can find the answers they need themselves. I will also briefly discuss the experience of belonging (which was the topic of my first book, *You Can Be Yourself Here*).

Let's start with a look at belonging.

CREATING A CLIMATE OF BELONGING

Back in the 1950s, management consultant and author Peter Drucker once famously said, "Culture will eat strategy for breakfast," and in doing so firmly placed corporate culture on the map and underlined how important culture is to the success of any company. Since then, an entire industry has arisen around the topic. In recent years, so important has the topic become that we are seeing C-suite-level culture roles and board interest in the culture of the companies they lead.

As someone who once held the role of chief learning

and culture officer, I of course espouse the significance and importance of culture. With that said, I also want to draw an important distinction between culture and climate.

I think of a company's culture as being the stated intentions, desires, and wishes the company articulates about the kind of company it is and the vibe it wants to create for its people, customers, and suppliers when they interact with each other. These intentions, wishes, and desires are usually laid out in a framework that I refer to as "cultural fabric," a.k.a. the vision, mission, values, and behaviors of an organization.

Then there is a company's climate, which is the actual lived experience employees have of the culture. The climate shows up in the way decisions are made, the way conflict is resolved, how people treat each other, how others are spoken about when they are not in the room, the way the company communicates about itself internally, the way those in management positions show up, and so on.

In an ideal world, you want your culture and your climate to overlap entirely, but realistically they are more likely to overlap in a Venn diagram kind of way. The bigger the intersection, the more likely the employees are to have a congruent and consistent experience of working there.

So, please accept my apologies, Mr. Drucker, because I have to disagree with you. It is not culture that will eat strategy for breakfast; it is, in fact, climate that will do that.

One factor of creating a climate of belonging is how inclusive that climate is.[16] Inclusion is a behavior, and that encompasses organizational behavior as well as individual behavior—organizational behavior being the policies, processes, products, frameworks, and protocols that are set up in an organization. An organization could have the most inclusive practices—it could have all the things I talk about in the first book, such as policies for trans people to transition, blind recruitment processes, and supportive technologies—but the culture will mean absolutely nothing and will not drive inclusion if the people in positions of leadership are not behaving in inclusive ways.

Said differently, the number one thing that will either

16   The other factor is diversity; you can see this formula in *You Can Be Yourself Here.*

promote or detract from inclusion is the way people in the positions of leadership behave. That includes everything from adhering to the policy process protocols that are set up to thinking about how they interact with other people and whether they are going to center the voices of people with identities that are not always centered, or behave in ways that are going to allow their unconscious biases to come into play.

INCREASED AWARENESS OF UNCONSCIOUS BIASES CONTRIBUTES TO A CULTURE OF BELONGING

I was once facilitating a group of senior people at an off-site, and during a breakout session I was moving among the three groups, each of which was standing by a flip chart. I walked up to one of the groups and I started to give them a pen so they could record their discussion on the flip chart. I caught myself about to hand the pen to the only woman in the group. I stopped myself and instead handed it to the most senior man in the group.

I prevented myself from playing into the tropes and stereotypes that either the most junior person or the woman should be taking notes. Fortunately, I caught myself in that moment so I could stop, but it made me wonder how many times I haven't caught or stopped that behavior. How many times have I, as a result of my own unconscious biases, played into the stereotypes or the social conditioning we receive as being part of the dominant culture—to put it bluntly, the cishet, white patriarchy?

Leaders must become increasingly aware of their unconscious biases, and the only way to do so is to do the work of understanding what those biases are, so they become conscious, and you can be aware of that influence when making decisions.

It can be very tempting, if we are not careful, to surround ourselves with like-minded others—those with similar skills, backgrounds, and experiences to us. After all, it feels safe, warm, and comforting to be with "people like us." However, this unconscious bias can cause leaders to build a team in their own likeness— the antithesis of diversity, inclusion, and belonging.

If your organization has not had this focus on creating a culture of belonging, enacting these changes may be uncomfortable. (Even if it has, creating these changes in *yourself* may be uncomfortable as well.) We know that change is necessary for growth, however, and so what becomes important is that a leader worth following manages that change, for themselves and for their team.

CHANGE MANAGEMENT REBRANDED

Mushrooms grow best when you keep them in the dark and feed them crap. This does not work for humans. They work best when they have context, access, and information. This does not mean you share anything and everything willy-nilly; caution and care are always important when communicating. But it does mean that transparency and openness are crucial if you want to be worth following.

When people say they love change, I don't believe them. Well, actually, I believe them with some skepticism because I think they're talking about specific types of change—that is, change they instigate. Change that we initiate, that we are in control of, and that we can manage is the kind of change that many people love, but change that is done to us, that we have little to no say over, that we are not in control of is fundamentally destabilizing and can be the cause of fear, uncertainty, or doubt.

If you have ever managed a desk move, you've likely quickly realized what can happen when you tell someone they're losing their window seat. Extrapolate that out into significant structural, procedural, or cultural change programs, and it is easy to see why things can quickly go wrong.

These days, if you aren't changing then you are going backward. Change is business as usual (BAU). We can't get away from it. But it isn't the change that you have to worry about. It's the emotional and psychological transition people will inevitably go through as a result of the changes they didn't choose.

Advances in neuroscience have shown us that the **not-instigated-by-us type of change fires up the same centers of the brain that light up when we are in physical pain.** This type of change is, quite literally, painful. It's no wonder we do whatever we can to resist it. We don't like pain and we'll go to extraordinary measures to avoid it.

In the words of Don Wilson, a participant in a leadership training I ran in 2018 in San Francisco, "I know that resistance to change can turn a good thing into a bad thing." Well said, Don.

This isn't new. People much more clever than me have talked about and written about these topics.

In 1969, Elisabeth Kübler-Ross wrote a groundbreaking book cheerily called *On Death and Dying*, in which she described the five stages of grief encountered by terminally ill patients. Her theories were quickly evolved to include any degree of personal loss, not just death, including the end of relationships, loss of job, and even small everyday personal losses not instigated by the individual. Empirically the model has yet to win the full support of psychologists, but it has been used time and again in the business world to chart the course of employees' engagement and performance in times of change while providing managers with some clues to action they can take to help people through the transition.

In the early 1990s, William Bridges published a book called *Managing Transitions*, which focused on the journey people go through as a result of change. He pointed out that change is gonna happen and change will happen quickly, but what doesn't happen quickly is the internal transition people have to make to adjust to the change. This happens much more slowly.

Needless to say, the introduction of any change to the

status quo that is not instigated by oneself will trigger an emotional journey. This emotional journey goes something like this:

Phase 1: Nah. When change is first announced, our initial emotional and cognitive waypoint is disbelief. This can show up in a number of ways, for example, refusing to engage with it, ignoring it until it goes away, or clinging onto a false reality hoping the change that's been communicated will go away. Nah can last a few days, or it can hang around for years. Ever heard someone say to you, "This place isn't like it used to be"? It's a sure sign they're still stuck somewhere in Nah as a result of a change at work.

Phase 2: OMG!! The two exclamation points are important. If (and I use the word "if" over "once" quite deliberately) people move beyond their states of disbelief, they allow themselves to feel their frustration and to think negative thoughts. This can show up as passive aggression, undermining, back channeling, or outright anger. Sometimes this can feel personally directed at you, but really it's just a manifestation of the brain pain they're experiencing. Companies and sectors that are allergic to emotion tend to try and stop OMG!! from happening, which just prolongs the transition and exacerbates the pain for everyone.

Phase 3: WTF? At some point, the anger will turn inward and morph into sadness or despair. Your people might start to feel like there is no point in railing against the change, that they have "no place" in the future of the organization, that maybe it's time for them to leave and find a place where they will once again feel settled and at home. Employee attrition will skyrocket as a result of WTF? if your transition is not being managed well.

Phase 4: Okay. This is not so much an agreement with the change, as in "It's okay," as it is an acceptance and recognition that the change is happening. When your people move into Okay, they're signaling their psychological resistance has diminished to a place from which they can now engage with the change; they can face and embrace an inevitable future.

These phases might happen sequentially, simultaneously, or they may even occur in some weird, random order, but they will happen. There is nothing that anyone can do to stop these steps from happening.

Therefore, the job of the leader(s) of any organization instigating the change is not to manage it per se, but rather to smooth the emotional and psychological transition by taking account of the Nah-OMG!!-WTF?-Okay response through the careful construction of some transition programming. Well-placed, thoughtfully thought-through employee experience activities will smooth the emotional bumps and melt the psychological barriers.

HOW TO TRAVEL SMOOTHLY THROUGH THE EMOTIONAL JOURNEY

How? Here's the annoying answer: it depends.

But really, it depends. And it depends on a number of factors—the size of the change, the size of your organization, the nature of the change (internal, external, or both), the culture of your organization and its readiness for transitions, the manner in which your leaders show up, and so on.

Here are a few top tips to whet your appetite:

- **Nah.** Repetition is key. Clearly sharing the Why of the change by articulating the current dissatisfaction (i.e., why the change is needed and what it is going to fix, add, or gain), what the change is, and how the change is going to happen.

- **OMG!!** The most effective antidote to the brain pain of OMG!! is patience. Organizations that are instigating change have a terrible habit of spending months, sometimes even years, planning changes and then expect their people to run toward the finish line in a matter of weeks. In this race toward the finish line, it's important to be the tortoise, not the hare. During OMG!! transition activities should center around giving space in one-on-one or group conversations for catharsis, and leaders are best served by not being surprised by, or taking personally, any emotional expression. They're going to happen, and it is much better to facilitate them happening in an open way than it is to let it go underground.

- **WTF?** Now is the time to listen with the intent to understand, not with the intent to reply. In the words of psychologist Carl Rogers, "When someone really hears you without passing judgment on you, without trying to take responsibility for you, without trying to mold you, it feels damn good...It is astonishing how elements that seem insoluble become soluble when someone listens, how confusions that seem irremediable turn into relatively clear flowing streams when one is heard."[17] When someone is WTF'ing, your one and only job is to listen deeply and acknowledge what you have heard. Don't try to reframe them, rescue them from their feelings, or encourage them with a "chin up." Once, and only once, you have listened deeply and understood what it is that you are hearing would it be appropriate to respond. Respond with what? A careful rearticulation of the Why and a sensitive, nonsalesy articulation of the benefits they might experience as a result of the change.

- **Okay.** This is the time to sell the change. Not in a rah-rah Pollyanna kind of way, but in a way that continues to paint the picture of What's in It for Me? (WIIFM). This is a time to double down on your efforts in articulating why this change will be beneficial for your people, your customers, and your business. It is also a really good time to start offering training on new processes and ways of working. If, through the change, teams are being restructured, now is the time to bring

17 Rogers, *A Way of Being*, 12.

people together for team development or team integration sessions—i.e., deliberate, facilitated moments through which new relationships and rapport can be built.

So, yes, change is BAU; it's necessary to ensure your brand establishes, maintains, and grows its position and reputation. The way you manage the transition will hold you back or it will accelerate your plans. With some careful thought and expert transition planning, you will have a seriously slick and humming culture ready to flex and adapt to anything.

COACHING

I'm sure you've heard the old adage, "Give a man a fish and he'll eat for a day, but teach a man to fish and he'll eat for life." Or perhaps you are familiar with the Benjamin Franklin quote, "Tell me and I forget; teach me and I may remember; involve me and I learn."

Coaching is about helping people find the answers within themselves to the challenges that they're facing.

Neuroscientific studies observing the social brain at work have shown that when people are enabled to figure out their own answers to complex problems, the neural activity in their brains is ten times higher than when somebody gives them the answer. So when somebody comes to you with a question and you give them the answer, they will have insight and they will have learned. Their synapses will fire and new neural connections will be made. On the other hand, if you are coached to arrive at the answer and you therefore have the experience of battling with it, struggling with it, chewing on it, and then finding the answer, the learning is generative because you not only learn, but you learn more than you can learn. Your self-efficacy is improved because you came up with the answer.

Leaders often ask me, "How do I get my team to stop asking me so many questions? If they weren't always asking me all these questions, I'd be able to get my own work done!"

And so I say to them, "Well, how good are you at answering the questions?"

"I'm really great at answering the questions."

"Then why would anyone stop coming to you when they know they're going to get an answer?"

Instead, I help those leaders learn how to apply basic coaching skills to their management practice. I'm not teaching people to become coaches—coaching is a skilled industry and it requires training and credentialing—but there are some basic concepts they can apply to bring a more coaching style to their leadership. This has the impact of helping that team learn and grow more rapidly, and freeing the leader up to no longer be an ATM dispensing answers every time an employee comes up and inserts that debit card of questions.

The challenge when using a coaching style comes when many managers say, "It's quicker if I just answer the question." They're right, it is quicker, but it will encourage learned helplessness. It will tell their people that they don't have to think for themselves, that they don't have to take risks, that they don't have to put themselves out there—their manager will do that for them. And so while it is quicker for the manager to answer, it is also self-defeating because the manager doesn't get to develop and grow beyond their current scope, and neither do the individuals. You end up with just a group of people who are overly dependent on each other rather than a team of people who can work together, grow together, and learn together.

HOW TO APPLY COACHING SKILLS
WHEN LEADING PEOPLE

The greatest coaches have a certain set of skills and beliefs, which we can examine and apply to your leadership skills. I've included some of the most important beliefs here.

PEOPLE HAVE ALL THE ANSWERS THEY
NEED INSIDE THEM ALREADY

First of all, they believe the other person has the answers inside of them; it's just a matter of creating the conditions for those answers to come out. So if, as a leader, I believe my answer is the only right answer, and my way is the right way, then I'm not going to be able to coach. I will be giving my team a fish instead of teaching them how to fish. So remember that people have the answers inside them, and it's your job as a manager to help them find the answer.

THE KEY TO FINDING THOSE ANSWERS IS ASKING GREAT QUESTIONS

The second belief is that coaching is just about asking really great questions, and really great questions start with who, what, where, when, and how.[18]

Any question that starts with *how* or *what* is going to generate present-moment awareness in the other person. *How* and *what* questions will help the individual tap into what happened and how it happened. Coaching can be about reviewing and processing something that has happened to gather the learnings, or can be about discussing something that is going to happen to help the individual be better prepared for it. So *how* and *what* answer not only what was happening or what is going to happen, but the strategies, the mental map, the mental processes that went into the decision they made or the output they delivered, or the decision they are going to make or output they are going to deliver.

One linguistic construction I find that people ask a lot, believing that they're asking a question, is called

---

18 Notice that I don't include the word *why*. This is intentional, because sometimes when the word *why* is used, it can imply blame and lead to justifications instead of answers.

a conversational postulate. This is a statement or a question that starts with, "Do you think…" or, "Don't you think…?" The problem with that is, yes, it is a question grammatically, but in actuality you are offering an opinion masquerading as a question. When you're in a position of power and you say, "Don't you think XYZ," don't you think most people will just agree with you? They will, because they are reading the meta-message behind that question, which is, "Here's my perspective; here's my opinion. Do you align with me?"

That conversational postulate is not coaching; it is telling people what you think they should think or do. That's a question designed essentially to have a yes or no answer.

Now, sometimes that's what you want. One of the principles I like to tell people is the quickest way to kill creativity is to let the leader speak first. As soon as the person in a position of power opens their mouth and offers an opinion or shares a perspective, the rest of the room starts to orient toward that outlook. (We'll look at how to solve this in just a moment.)

SIMPLY FOCUS ON GREEN AND RED

The next coaching skill you can apply is, when you are reviewing someone's performance or deliverable, to encourage the deepest amount of learning, focus on green and red and not on white.

What does that mean? Green, which is the universal color for go, means performance and output that is above expectations. Red, which is the universal symbol for stop, is for performance and delivery that didn't meet expectations. White, which is the color for surrender, is for performance that meets expectations. The idea here is that you place attention and focus on how to make the green repeatable and how to make the red avoidable in the future.

I encourage you to introduce the green, red, and white terminology with your team. I introduced this concept when I was the head of organizational development at a travel and tourism organization I worked with in the early 2000s. The CEO and executive team said to me, "We're never going to use green and red; we're just gonna tell it how it is."

A year after introducing this terminology, the entire organization was talking in green, red, and white when reviewing performance because it just *made sense*. When you use the words "below expectation" or "didn't meet expectations," that feels heavier than using the word red, and so it just becomes a nice vernacular to use.

The principle is not to focus on performance and delivery that is at the expected level. When you're coaching, focus on what is above expectation and what didn't meet expectations.

YOU-ME-AGREE

The next coaching skill to learn is using You-Me-Agree. This is the antidote to what I previously mentioned, which is that the quickest way to kill creativity is for the leader to speak first. Instead, in every conversation that is about performance with the individual—that is, a performance development review, coaching, or even giving feedback—using this principle says that the direct report or team member always speaks first.

If I were coaching you, dear reader (I'll call you DR for short), I would say to you, "So, DR, we were in that client meeting an hour ago. I'd love to unpack and explore that with you and gather the learnings with you. Let's review your performance. In that meeting, what did you do that was green?"

You would share, and I would listen and nod and affirm, but I wouldn't give my opinion at all. Then I would say, "And what about red, DR? What, for you, didn't meet expectations?"

Again, you would share. And again, I would nod and I would affirm, and then I would have my turn. I might say, "DR, I hear that A, B, and C were green for you. I'd like to add D as well, as being green. Here's what I heard you say was red: X, Y, and Z. I think you're being a little bit unfair to yourself on one of those. And actually, here's something that you didn't mention that I picked up on."

With You-Me-Agree, you offer your perspective and opinions first. Once you are done, I would share my perspective, then we would have a conversation about your perspective and my perspective, and we would come to some form of agreement. If we can come to some form of agreement, we'll come to some form of alignment.

RAISING THE BAR

Raising the bar means thinking about coaching the individual, not coaching the job role.

You could have a team of people who are all performing the same role—let's say, for example, you are managing a team of five project managers who all share the same job title and the same set of accountabilities. They are also five very different human beings with different skills, outlooks, values, behaviors, and experiences. It is shortsighted to try to coach them against their job description.

Coaching against them as a person means you focus on the individual and notice what is green for them might not be green for everybody else. What is red for them might not be red for everybody else. And likewise with white performance, because I might be a project manager with the same accountabilities and I have five years of experience, or I might be a project manager with the same accountabilities and have two years of experience. I should be coached and treated differently in terms of my performance.

To take this one step further, if you're coaching the individual and not the job title, then what is green today will be white tomorrow, and what's white today will be red tomorrow, because the bar raises as you gather more skills, more experience, and more miles on the clock.

EXAMPLES OF THE IMPORTANCE OF CREATING CONDITIONS FOR YOUR PEOPLE TO BE SUCCESSFUL

From JW: When I started at my current company in Canada, inclusion was one of the words I used to describe the way I would manage the business. As an immigrant, I had been subjected to the "well, you don't have local experience" routine, and I was determined to break that approach. I was also starting from scratch, so I needed to persuade people to join a small fledgling company (with a massive backer, but still...) and take on projects that were going to be challenging. The people I hired have always stepped up to fill in the holes when others have struggled and were the drivers for us winning one of the biggest infrastructure projects in Canadian history.

This year my board gave everyone a "coronavirus" and a "work from home" bonus to say thank you. I shared my whole bonus with the team without telling them. If they knew, they would say it was not necessary, but to me it was. They are the stars. When I told my boss, he said, "Well, that is very noble but you didn't need to do that."

On the flip side, my boss has been textbook in creating a situation of isolation. Last year, after another bad year of financial performance, he came up with another idea: reorganization! Unfortunately my group was to be moved from one company to another company, which is not an easy move and doesn't happen overnight, plus requires multiple boards to agree. Before the groundwork was complete, I was removed from meetings, updates, and briefings—all while the company we were to be moved under refused to support us, as their board had not agreed to the move!

This has led to a situation of isolation, and while the impact on the team has been minor (because I was open in briefings about how it would work, i.e., very little change), for me it has been massive. I have been upset, angry, and at times have wanted to walk away because of the treatment. During my performance review I was open and told my boss I felt excluded and isolated, and he apologized. But then recently, when the CEO of the group came to visit Canada, my boss, who is here to "oversee" this newly won project, had a "core team dinner" and didn't include me, even though I am head of the country! It might seem petty, but it felt like access was being restricted to the CEO to ensure the message was managed and he was kept unaware of the reality and the challenges. In the grand scheme of things it doesn't matter—a friend's husband had a heart attack and another mutual friend lost her dad; all I did was not get invited to a dinner—but the way you make other people feel creates long-term success.

From AH: Truly putting the people over the business, through using inclusive language and inclusive thought partners from various backgrounds, will make the company thrive in the long run. It allows employees to feel seen and valued and invest themselves into a company, cutting back on time lost training with constant new hires. I've seen companies falter in this area and spend more time training and less time evolving and retaining, leaving everyone frustrated and feeling unsupported.

From K: This is a principle I live by aggressively. I have always believed that most of business is not about business, but about people and their lives. I make it a point to prioritize people's experiences, their development, their path, and their enjoyment of the work over the profit of the company. The result has been a culture that is very close to family (even though I know companies can never really be families). More than that, when I do this, it always seems as if the profit follows. We work so well, and our quality is so high, that clients want to work with us.

When a leader creates the conditions for success, that's exactly what follows...more success for everyone—the individual, the leader, the team, and the organization. And once you get a taste of that success, everyone will be hungry for more. But how can others learn from those leaders? Chapter 10 shows how leaders who are worth following are also worth copying.

CHAPTER 10

LEADERS WHO ARE WORTH FOLLOWING...ARE WORTH COPYING

One evening, when my husband, Davis, and I were living in London in the early 2000s, we were babysitting our very young goddaughter, Stella.

Davis and I were in the kitchen preparing Stella some dinner, and Stella was off in the corner playing with our two dogs, Penny and Twinkle. Out of nowhere, we heard this little angelic voice say, "For f*ck's sake, Twinkle, eat the biscuit!"

I looked at Davis.

Davis looked at me.

And I said to Davis, "Where the f*ck did she get that language from?"

BEHAVIOR IS CONTAGIOUS

It is important to remember that you are always role-modeling something. Anyone who has young people in their life will know how quickly we mimic and copy and pick up on the behaviors of those around us. We can't *not* do it.

So the question is, are you walking the kind of walk and speaking the kind of talk that you want others to emulate? Because they will. You see, your behavior is contagious. We are wired to copy each other. It's just one of the ways we learn, develop, and grow.

In our early years we copy our parents, older siblings, and primary caregivers. At school age, we model our teachers and our peer group, and as we professionally mature, we tend to adopt the behaviors and ways of working from those who are senior to us.

In my first book, I laid out how high school and the world of work have a lot in common. So too do primary caregivers and parents have a lot in common with managers and leaders, because they both occupy a position of power. So we are hardwired to copy other human beings, and we are further influenced by the human beings who have power over us, which means that one of the ways we will find to belong is to align with and to model the behaviors of other people who are in power over us.

This means that our behavior as leaders is more powerful than we may think, and equally important is how we use that power.

IMPACT VERSUS INTENTION

It was Stephen Covey who said, "We judge ourselves by our intentions and we judge others by their behavior," and in doing so emphasized the importance of behavior and the way it impacts others, especially those we lead.

Good intentions are not enough when it comes to being a leader worth following. The workforce today, rightly, demands more from the people who hold these positions; they expect good intentions to be turned into positive impact, and they expect leaders to take accountability when their impact is off. Given the emphasis on relation over task that often comes with leadership positions, I like to share the following quote from Vienna Pharoan, a licensed marriage and family therapist based out of New York City:

> Just because your intentions are good doesn't mean that you aren't impacting people negatively. We can always mean well, but if we don't slow down to consider how our words, decisions, and behaviors impact those around us, we run the risk of doing some serious harm. Make the impact just as important as your intentions and see how your relationships begin to change.

I believe the behavior of people who we think of as leaders, or as being senior to us, is likely to have a greater influence on our behavior than any other people we work with. I have also come to believe that relationships and the way we behave with each other is the wellspring of any organizational culture.

How we interact with each other as we do our work, how we talk to each other, what we say about other people when they are not in the room, and particularly how we treat each other in times of stress, conflict, and overwhelm all impact culture in deeply profound and systemic ways.

Leaders who focus more on their impact than their well-meaning intentions are worth following because they make sure their behavior is worth copying. They don't talk a good talk; instead, they ensure demonstration is the teacher.

BAD BEHAVIOR IS CONTAGIOUS, TOO

I also believe that a company's climate[19] is most significantly influenced by the people who hold leadership positions—and would go further to say that the climate is shaped by the worst behavior you are willing to tolerate in your leaders. Relationships and the way people treat each other are the wellspring of any culture.

If you think about a manager, they can hold the keys to the car for many things: for an individual, they hold the promotion keys; they hold the task-delegation

---

19   See Chapter 9 for my explanation of the difference between culture and climate.

keys; they hold the keys to whether you are included or not, or whether you get a pay rise or not. Here we are as human beings with a hardwired predisposition to copying other people who are further influenced by power. When you have a manager who is sitting in a leadership position, their behavior is going to both overtly and covertly, consciously and unconsciously influence the behavior of everybody around them. What we see becomes acceptable, because we think that's the way things are going to get done. If we do what they do, we will get by.

Therefore, the worst behavior we're willing to tolerate in a leader is what is going to drive the organizational climate or the team climate. It's going to drive the day-to-day interactions and relationships. We all want to think we're only copying the "good" behaviors or the best behaviors, but the reality is that we're going to copy *any* behaviors from a person in power. And if a leader is doing it, then it must be acceptable to do it that way—even if it means impacting people in a negative way.

So if the worst set of behaviors that you're willing to tolerate are what drive the change in the company, the goal here is to change those sets of behaviors and to lay out the set of behaviors that are part of good leadership. The goal is to be a leader who is worth copying, which means being a decent human being.

If you show up as a decent human being, then chances are everyone around you is going to model that—and *that* is why leaders who are worth following are worth copying.

LIMITING BELIEFS OF LEADERS

If values govern all behavior, then beliefs govern our perception and our process of meaning-making (which was discussed in Chapter 2). This is true for both positive and negative, or limiting, beliefs.

Occupational psychology research has shown that around 56 percent of leaders experience some self-limiting beliefs that could be holding them back from fulfilling their full underlying potential.

Self-limiting beliefs show up as the inner voices that can cripple us with doubt, sabotage our well-being, keep us awake at night, and get in the way of us operating at our very best.

Some very common self-limiting beliefs are:

- "Everything's got to be perfect." This is your inner perfectionist talking to you, which can often be useful, but sometimes their voice gets just a bit too loud! When this happens, leaders put undue pressure on themselves to be totally flawless. The maladaptive form of the perfectionist leads to massive self-imposed pressure to achieve unrealistic goals, which sets up the leader (and their stakeholders) for repeated disappointment. Leaders who run this belief can be their own worst critics, which can be damaging to self-esteem and overlay harsh criticism of others.

- "I'm going to get found out." The nagging fear and doubt that you are not up to the job is also known as imposter syndrome. Leaders who run this belief tend to have lots of underlying anxiety and self-doubt. This tendency is often seen in highly diligent and capable female leaders who can feel the need to work much harder than others to "cover up" for perceived (but not real) deficiencies. Always trying to keep up this impression of supreme competence, together with feeling anxious about being found out, can prove utterly exhausting.

- "I cannot let go of the detail." Leaders who have a

strong need for control tend to run this belief. This is a person who is really struggling to step away from the operational detail to take a more strategic perspective. Often this is because the leader's self-worth has been bolstered from their competence at years of successful execution. This can be a real concern for leaders who need to occupy roles where results are harder to measure and in a context where the leader has no reputation or track record to rely on.

- "What will they think of me if it goes wrong?" This belief stems from a fear of failure. The underlying emotion driving this belief is self-consciousness and, in extreme cases, a sense of shame—emotions that can really damage self-confidence and knock self-esteem. Often a leader with a powerful fear of failure may avoid taking risks or trying out new ideas and dislikes learning new skills because it leaves them anxious about making mistakes.

Self-awareness and identifying the limiting belief is the first step.

The next step is self-acceptance—i.e., simply allowing that belief to exist. I acknowledge that this might seem counterintuitive, but bear with me here while I explain. It's most likely that uncovering a limiting belief also comes with some uncomfortable feelings[20] that you likely don't want to feel. To that end, you might be drawn into an internal struggle in which you try to obliterate, resist, or quash the belief. But the problem with this approach is that this limiting belief was probably developed by you at a point in time for *very* good reasons. If this is the case, you're not very likely, at an unconscious level, to want to give up that belief.

A lot of my work with people—both clinically and in coaching settings—involves this process of acceptance. Why? A couple of reasons. First, the Paradoxical Theory of Change[21] tells us that when people allow themselves to be fully aware and in touch with who they currently are, change and growth then emerge as the inevitable and natural outcome of such contact and genuine self-knowledge. We know that what we resist often persists, so self-acceptance can often dissolve, rather than resolve, a problem.

Whether you prefer self-reflection as a means of learning and growth, or you decide to engage a coach or

---

20 Such as anger, shame, guilt, fear, and/or disappointment.

21 A philosophy that comes from Gestalt psychology.

partner with a trusted colleague to support you, the final step when working with limiting beliefs is self-development. That is to say, engaging in a process to develop your understanding of the role and purpose the limiting belief had (or still has), the undesired impact it has in your life today, and the empowering beliefs you would like to adopt instead.

EXAMPLES OF THE IMPORTANCE OF BEING WORTH COPYING

From AH: I've always believed it's better to lead with action, "walk the talk," and set the tone of what you expect of your employees by modeling that behavior. I've done that with my teams, from scrubbing toilets with them, to how I talk to clients, to how I talk to fellow team members, and to how I lead with empathy and a positive and inclusive mindset. I've had leaders who simply delegated to me but lost my trust that they actually practiced the behavior they expected of their team, and it leaves me untrusting of my managers.

From XH: It can be very damaging when a manager can't control their emotional impulses and vents their frustrations on the people working with them. The behavior sometimes is not as professional as expected, and those moments erode trust in the working relationships.

From K: My previous company was one I loved. The people were bright, intellectual, and inclusive. It was one of the best jobs I ever had. And my boss was honestly one of the best bosses I ever had. He was always willing to share his approach with me, why he made decisions about the business the way he did, and how he decided to start and grow the business.

However, there were times when it felt like the way he financially managed the business was at odds with the culture he created. He wasn't greedy or unethical, but it felt as though he prioritized certain financial measures that felt at odds with our culture of openness. Culturally, it felt like we all had an influence on the direction of the company; financially, it felt like they were only his decisions to make. I think technically they were, but the dissonance felt odd when it came up.

From AS: I've had bad leaders and good leaders, and both stick with you as learning experiences. Always remember how you felt when someone wasn't respectful, courteous, or driven. Then make sure you never emulate that behavior. I've learned as much from those I didn't believe in as those

I did. The leaders that inspired, cultivated, and cared are still my friends to this day. The mutual respect and admiration is a bond that I pride myself on developing. I always want to be an accessible, understanding, clear, concise, and inspirational leader. What you project, others pick up!

From NS: I hate to use the term rule book, but there are certain guide rails my team knows I expect of them, and for them to expect of each other.

1. I bring me—all of me—to each team meeting.

2. No idea is a bad idea, even if it's not right for right now.

3. I share feedback with positive intent.

4. For the time we spend together in this meeting, everything else is secondary.

The impact is that everyone is invested in that time together. We pool our energy and our talents to create magic. We add, we shape, and we squeeze every drop of brilliance we can from a plan. The best bit? We do it all together.

Now that you know others are picking up what you're putting out there...are you becoming someone worth following *and* copying? If so, you are well on your way. But your leadership journey isn't over yet. Chapter 11 holds you accountable because leaders who are worth following don't walk by.

CHAPTER 11

LEADERS WHO ARE WORTH FOLLOWING... DON'T WALK BY

From CD: Early on in my new job, I remember sitting with my manager at a table outside in San Francisco. We were having a catch-up, and I don't remember what happened, but I started crying in front of him for the first time. I was pretty mortified.

My manager truly rose to the occasion, though, and I remember him meeting my vulnerability with some vulnerable shares of his own. It made me feel super supported and safe, and I think about that moment to this day. I have no idea what we were talking about anymore, but the fact that I can still remember him holding space for me means a lot.

YOU ARE ACCOUNTABLE

Leaders who are worth following hold themselves and others to account and they demonstrate that accountability is a verb, and not just a noun. They focus on performance. They don't walk by and, if something needs doing, fixing, or changing, they take care of it. Or they bring the right people together to do it, fix it, or change it.

ACCOUNTABILITY THE NOUN VERSUS ACCOUNTABILITY THE ACTION

Leaders who are worth following hold themselves and others to account. Just as leadership is a behavior, not a title, accountability is an action, not a noun.

Of course the noun type of accountability does exist—in the form of **Responsible, Accountable, Supporting, Consulted, and Informed** (RASCI), job descriptions, process matrices, and all the other paraphernalia designed to get people to do what you want them to do. But the truth of the matter is people don't do what they're told. They do what they are shown, which is why the action type of accountability is so important. Leaders who model this type of accountability don't walk by, in that if something needs doing, fixing, or changing, they will personally take care of it (or they will bring the right people together to do it, fix it, or change it).

I hear leaders in a lot of organizations say, "We have an accountability problem."

First of all, I like to help them to notice whether they really have an accountability problem or not, which means differentiating between accountability the noun and accountability the action. If you say you have an accountability problem, the first place I would ask anyone to go is to check your org charts, your job descriptions, any RASCIs, or statements of responsibility. Is it clear enough? Is there role clarity within those statements? If so, you don't have an accountability-the-noun problem.

From there, you have to make sure you have clearly articulated role-level responsibilities and team-level responsibilities. As discussed previously, the first step is role clarity and the next step is role acceptance.

If you've got role clarity, you better check that you've got role acceptance as well. It's not just a matter of making sure your job descriptions are clear; you have to go through a process of making sure that everybody not only knows their responsibilities but also accepts them and therefore accepts other people's responsibilities. Organizations and teams can often suffer from people swimming outside their lane or people not swimming fully in their own lane.

If you don't have an accountability-the-noun problem, you might have an accountability-the-action problem, which you can check using the flower of accountability in the next section.

THE FLOWER OF ACCOUNTABILITY

Let's take a closer look at each piece of the flower of accountability, as shown in the following image.

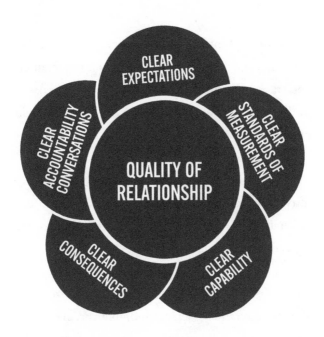

Clear expectations: The expectations must be clearly articulated, understood, and accepted by the person being held to account.

Clear standards of measurement: The standard, level, or degree to which the work must be delivered must be clearly articulated, understood, and accepted by the person being held to account.

Clear capability: The person being held to account must have the skills, knowledge, and experience to deliver on the expectations to the required standards.

Clear consequences: The consequences of delivering and of not delivering the accountability to expectations and standards required should be clearly articulated, understood, and accepted by the person being held to account.

Clear accountability conversations: Follow-up must routinely happen and consequences should be enacted. This is true of meeting and not meeting expectations and standards.

Quality of relationship: The quality of the relationship between the person accountable and the person holding them to account is the fuel that drives the accountability framework. The quality of the relationship between the individual and their actual work is also crucial here.

Quality of relationship is very purposely in the center of the flower. Notice that when I say quality of relationship, I don't mean the quality of the likability between the person being held to account and the person holding to account. I mean the quality of rapport—the energetic projection of trust, respect, and interest. So the quality of the relationship that exists is my ability to assume positive intent, my ability to give other people the benefit of the doubt, and the extent to which I'm going to feel psychologically safe in this relationship.

And that has nothing to do with reporting lines. There are so many organizations and teams these days that work in matrix structures where there are multiple reporting lines, and somebody will say, "I don't have a direct reporting line over this person, so it's hard for me to be able to get things done through them or with them." I always call bullshit on that, because the more senior you get in an organization, the more influence without direct power you have to be able to have. It isn't about having a line on an org chart, because that really and truly only means something to a certain extent.

People these days don't do what they're told to do. They do what they want to do. And the extent to which we are influenced to do what we want to do will be colored by the quality of the rapport and relationship we have with the person that is asking us to do something.

When you wake up in the morning, go to work, get to your desk, open your laptop, and look at your inbox to see that anywhere between ten and 150 emails have come in since you logged off yesterday, I bet that the first emails you go to will be those from the people you have a good level of rapport and a good quality of relationship with. (And the last emails you'll go to are from people that you don't.) That's why quality of relationship is right at the center of that flower, because it fuels the rest of them.

Allow me to share with you a quote from a leader I was working with recently, upon being introduced to the flower of accountability: "I didn't buy it when you called it the flower of accountability. It seemed too soft for something that is a hard issue for our business. But when I got into it and used it as a framework and a model to manage a conversation with my leadership team, I found it not only to be a learning moment about my colleagues, but also a little window into myself. I am not only grateful for this model, I now find it an invaluable part of all my discussions and interactions with my team."

That shows the mindset that some people have when looking at this specific model, but perhaps when looking at the larger concepts as well. They think, "Well, that's just cute," until they actually start putting some of these into place and see the difference it can make, not just with our teams, but within ourselves.

EXAMPLES OF THE IMPORTANCE
OF NOT WALKING BY

From JW: When I first came over to Canada, I worked for a consultancy who were fully happy to let me work myself into the ground or burn out. As long as the money was rolling in, no one cared or did anything about the ever-increasing bad behavior until it came to a head and I was taking long-term sick leave and on the verge of quitting.

From AS: I once had a leader that would yell at us. This actually demotivated everyone, and in the end we all resigned. No one was willing to accept this behavior, yet the company never took action. The lesson here is that you will lose good employees if they are not valued and respected.

From AH: Feedback in the moment is one of the most important things I've learned in past companies, but only if it's practiced. When put into practice, we get a stronger, more inclusive work environment where everyone feels safe. See something, say something—even if you're unsure if it's "allowed" or said in the right words.

Not only do leaders who are worth following not walk by, but as you'll see in Chapter 12, they take it one step further: they bring their people with them.

CHAPTER 12

LEADERS WHO ARE WORTH FOLLOWING... BRING THEIR PEOPLE WITH THEM

Reflect for a moment on these two scenarios taken from a workplace you may, or may not, recognize:

Scenario #1: The alarm goes off on Monday morning at 5:00 a.m. You have had a restless night's sleep after a helluva weekend in which the family troubles that have been bubbling finally boiled over and the weather was a pile of poop, which meant no one could get outside and were under each other's feet all weekend. To cap it all off, you and your partner had a big ole falling out on Sunday night, which meant you weren't able to get to the report you had promised yourself you would finish over the weekend in favor of an on-time finish on Friday evening.

You open up your calendar and log into Zoom for the first meeting of the day, which is, as always, the weekly team meeting in which each team member walks through the report that describes last week's business performance.

You just can't bring yourself to smile and act as if everything is okay, so you decide to go camera-off this week. As everyone logs on and chats cheerily about their weekend, your boss opens the meeting with a quick go-round-the-room, checking in with everyone before getting stuck into the report review. The creeping-death-of-check-ins finally reaches you, and you muster all the strength and courage to say, "The weekend was fine. I'm fine. Everything is fine. Thanks." By the tone of your voice, everyone in the room can tell you're not fine (as if the camera-off wasn't already a telltale sign).

Your boss quickly moves on, silently worrying that if they dwell too long on you, the mood will be brought down and everyone else will start to feel not okay. For the rest of the meeting you're distracted, still with one foot in the weekend chewing over the argument you had last night. When it comes to the part of the meeting when you present your performance report, you go as quickly as you can, offering as little as you can to get by, and you stay off camera.

The next time you hear from your boss is toward the end of the week, in a team-wide email reminding everyone that the reports are due and they will be reviewed in the weekly team meeting on Monday.

Scenario #2: The alarm goes off on Monday morning at 5:00 a.m. You have had a restless night's sleep after a helluva weekend in which the family troubles that have been bubbling finally boiled over and the weather was a pile of poop, which meant no one could get outside and were under each other's feet all weekend. To cap it all off, you and your partner had a big ole falling out on Sunday night, which meant you weren't able to get to the report you had promised yourself you would finish over the weekend in favor of an on-time finish on Friday evening.

You open up your calendar and log into Zoom for

the first meeting of the day, which is, as always, the weekly team meeting in which each team member walks through the report that describes last week's business performance.

You just can't bring yourself to smile and act as if everything is okay, so you decide to go camera-off this week. As everyone logs on and chats cheerily about their weekend, your boss opens the meeting with a quick go-round-the-room, checking in with everyone before getting stuck into the report review. The creeping-death-of-check-ins finally reaches you and you muster all the strength and courage to say, "The weekend was fine. I'm fine. Everything is fine. Thanks." By the tone of your voice, everyone in the room can tell you're not fine (as if the camera-off wasn't already a telltale sign).

Your boss pauses, takes a breath, and says, "Thanks for sharing, everyone. I know sometimes it is hard to kick into gear for these Monday morning meetings. I appreciate you all being here." With your boss's words, you notice your nervous system settling slightly and you feel more able to be present with the rest of the team. While you stay off camera for the rest of the meeting, you confidently present your report and are even open and receptive to some questions from the rest of the team about one line item that didn't perform as well as the others.

Soon after the meeting, you receive a ping from your boss who thanks you for showing up today and offers up some time to check in one-on-one if you would like to. They are careful to let you know it is not for anything in particular; it's just that they noticed you weren't your usual self earlier that day, that they don't wish to pry, but that they are here for you and willing to listen if there is anything you want to share. While you don't respond immediately to your boss's message, you notice that you feel fortunate for being part of this team and increasingly more able to engage with work after such a shitty weekend.

LIFT YOUR PEOPLE UP

Which of the two leaders in the previous scenarios is one you would want to follow?

Everybody wants to know they are cared for and their development is important. Leaders who adopt a coaching style to their management practice, who lead with empathy, and who give their people the benefit of the doubt will engender followership because this will show how much they care about their people, their work, and their careers.

Receiving an empathetic response will result in team members being more effective; it's an important part of proactively managing discretionary effort.[22] The knock-on effect on the rest of the team is also worth noting, as the responses from the boss in each scenario will communicate to the broader team certain messages about what is, and what is not, okay around here.

Leaders who are worth following will bring their people with them through hard human kindness, empathy, and vulnerability, each of which we will explore in more detail in this chapter.

SHIFT HAPPENS THROUGH
HARD HUMAN KINDNESS

Hard human kindness is an upgrade to what some folks call "tough love," and it has a deliberate intention of moving the leader more toward their optimal out-

---

22 You can read more about this in the Soul Trained article entitled "What Is the Most Important Tool in Your Management Kit Bag?" available at this website: https://soul-trained.medium.com/what-is-the-most-important-tool-in-your-management-kit-bag-c4d4cf8c1bcb

comes. One key component underpinning the delivery of this is the ability to lead with empathy; a behavior that is nonnegotiable if you want to be a leader who is worth following.

In recent months, the topic of empathy seems to have been talked about more than ever, and in a 2018 *Forbes* article, Javier Pladevall, the CEO of VW Audi Retail in Spain, is quoted as saying, "Leadership today is about unlearning management and relearning being human." I couldn't agree more. It feels like the tide is at last turning on previous cynical attitudes toward "soft skills" as being associated with weak leaders who are too nice and just want to make you feel good.

In fact, I reject the use of the word "soft" in relation to empathetic leadership; instead I prefer to talk about "relational skills," or better yet Daniel Goleman's concept of emotional intelligence. I believe the behavioral side of being in a people-management role actually takes enormous strength, and without serious amounts of empathy, you will not encourage followership.

Let's take a closer look at what we really mean when we talk about empathy and why we believe it's so important.

First, a definition. Empathy is the ability to understand someone else's feelings and the ability to communicate (through words and behaviors) your understanding. It's important to note that there is a distinction between sympathy (feeling *for* someone) and empathy (feeling *with* someone).

In fact, according to Carl Rogers, the founder of person-centered therapy and author of *On Becoming a Person*, "Empathy is the listener's effort to hear the other person deeply, accurately, and nonjudgmentally. Empathy involves skillful, reflective listening that clarifies and amplifies the person's own experience and meaning, without imposing the listener's own material."

HOW TO HAVE MORE EMPATHY

Like kindness, empathy doesn't cost a penny, but the ROI is incredible. Brené Brown says that empathy is a skill, which means it is something we can all learn to do. Here are some quick tips on how to bring about greater empathy in your leadership.

I.   **Assume positive intent:** This is not the same as letting people walk all over you, nor is it the same as letting people off the hook, and it certainly isn't about not holding others to account for their behavior. The act of assuming positive intent is a conscious process of recognizing and remembering that we are all doing the best we can with the resources we have available to us at the time, that none of us get up in the morning to come to work to do a deliberately bad job. Notice what happens to the way you approach problem situations or conflict in team relationships when you start from a place of assuming positive intent. It will change your life.

2. **Give the benefit of the doubt:** When we give people the benefit of the doubt by suppressing our suspicions (until proven otherwise), we demonstrate that we respect their model of the world and we show up as someone who is interested, curious, and open. Giving the benefit of the doubt is a posture of softening, and solving problems from this place is infinitely easier and more enjoyable for all concerned.

3. **Meet people where they are at:** Or, as we like to say at Soul Trained, meet people at their bus stop. What do we mean by that? Simply, instead of

trying to convince your people that your way is the right way, take a moment or two to explore, unpack, and respect where they are coming from and the many ways in which they interpret the world. See how quickly your people grow and improve their performance when you meet them where they are at, instead of having them meet you where you are at.

4. **Listen with the intent to understand:** The late great Stephen Covey (author of *The Seven Habits of Highly Effective People*) is known to have said that most people don't listen with the intent to understand; they listen with the intent to reply. We'll say this loud for the people at the back—THIS IS NOT REALLY LISTENING! You see, when we are listening with the intent to reply, we are doing what is known as "queueing" or, in other words, we are **waiting to talk**. We're up in our heads, perhaps formulating a clapback, a clever question, or a rebuttal to react to a portion of what someone else has just said. *No bueno*. You cannot truly listen while waiting to talk. It's as simple as that.

VULNERABILITY

Until the power of vulnerability was thrust into the mainstream by Brené Brown, it used to be viewed as a trait of the weak, so it simply wasn't talked about.

Being a hard-nosed, strong-minded, ball-busting leader was promoted by, and projected into, everyday business culture. The slightest sign of weakness could damage your reputation and diminish your power and authority.

In business we are actively encouraged to talk about successes and positive outcomes and to never mention our fears, doubts, or mistakes. If you wanted to be perceived as courageous and successful, you could never be seen as vulnerable.

Oh, how wrong we were.

Vulnerability is a seriously important power tool in the tool kit of a leader who is worth following. Being vulnerable can help you process your emotions rather than brushing them under the carpet only to have them pop up and manifest in other ways. It helps you maintain a level of emotional equilibrium and it fosters mental health.

I have often said that relationships are the wellspring of any workplace climate (climate being the implicit culture and the actual lived experience of employees—which may or may not be different from the explicitly stated and intended culture). The way we treat each other, the way we talk about others when they are not in the room, and the way we come together to deal with conflict and pressure drives the climate. Vulnerability helps you relate with and be relatable to others; it helps you to show up as a human *being* rather than as a human *doing,* and it will allow your people to connect with you. In other words, it will help you become a leader worth following.

You cannot deny, nor can you escape, the truth revealed by not only Brené Brown's work, but the reams and reams of research that tell us that vulnerability is a must-have skill for leaders to nurture.

THE BENEFITS OF BEING VULNERABLE

What does it mean to "be vulnerable"? I am not talking about trust falls, nor am I talking about kumbaya by the campfire, and neither am I talking about the need to talk about your trials and tribulations all the time.

No, I am talking about the courageous type of vulnerability, the type that, as Susan Jeffers reminds us, guides us to feel the fear and do it anyway; this is the type of vulnerability that powers you on, even when you are unsure, uncertain, or unclear.

The type of vulnerability that gives you permission to talk about your not-so-successful endeavors and decisions you made can actually be very powerful. Your team will find the transparency refreshing, as it makes them feel better about themselves to know other people, especially the person they follow, who doesn't always "have it all together."

In early 2022, in a survey of over twelve thousand global employees, Catalyst revealed that people are more willing to go the extra mile at work when their manager is open and shows vulnerability. The report went on to show that these employees tend to be more creative, dedicated, and willing to go "above and beyond." Leaders who show vulnerability and empathy are stronger, not weaker. Their teams tend to feel psychologically safer, and to express themselves more freely without fear of making mistakes.

The term "psychological safety" wasn't coined until 1965 by Schein and Bennis, and was then applied to the workplace in 1990 by William Kahn. Psychological safety is a function of respect and permission and occurs when people feel as though it is not expensive to be themselves.

In 2016, Google's Project Aristotle proved that IQ and resources cannot compensate for an absence of psychological safety. Based on this study, I believe that psychological safety is the single most important factor contributing to workplace performance.

When people feel psychologically safe at work, they are able to say things like:

- I don't know.

- I made a mistake.

- I disagree.

- I might be wrong.

- I am sorry.

- I have a concern.

- You are right.

- I have an idea.

When people don't feel safe, they won't say those things. And if they don't get to say those things, it's clear to see the impact it will have on workplace performance and engagement:

- If you can't share your ideas, that comes at the cost of innovation.

- If you can't say, "I don't know," that comes at the cost of expensive errors.

- If you can't say, "I might be wrong," that comes at the cost of inviting other people into the conversation.

- If you can't say you have a concern, that comes at the cost of further wrongdoing and further threatening the psychological safety of the team or group.

But, again, when you are able to say those things, the reverse applies:

- When you can say, "I don't know," you are making yourself available for learning and help.

- When you can say you have an idea, and that idea is listened to, then you open yourself up to innovation, change, and creativity.

- When you say, "I may have made a mistake," you open yourself to fallibility, humanity, and the ability to stop underperforming in the future.

- If you are able to say, "I disagree," then you open yourself to the possibility that what you're about to do can be even greater than it is.

Being able to say all of these in one way or another leads to greater cohesion because you're learning from other people. You're communicating your ideas with other people. You are expressing your mistakes and perhaps getting help, again from other people. You're innovating together.

EXAMPLES OF THE IMPORTANCE OF
BRINGING YOUR PEOPLE WITH YOU

From AS: I'm currently working for a CEO who believes we work "for him," not "with him." This has created a culture of lack of trust and value. When we are told, "I'm the CEO" at the start of a sentence, it doesn't elicit the response he's actually looking for. In fact, it does the opposite and makes you question his ability to lead, cultivate, and grow a company and its talent.

From AH: I always try to lift up my team when I'm given praise. If a leader or teammate praises me on a job well done, I use that moment to lift up those that supported me or contributed in ways that were necessary to move the work forward. Nothing feels worse than when someone takes credit for your hard work, especially a manager.

From XH: I know somebody who has gathered a small crowd of followers through the years. The people in the field respect his opinion and would join his next adventure when opportunities arise. In turn, he would promote or refer his network to positions he sees fit. It speaks volumes of the leader's effectiveness and caring nature.

From K: I had a direct report who was feeling stressed. Our company was running a lot of projects, and we all had more than we could really handle. Part of my job, aside from running projects as well, was to keep tabs on this team. I had to navigate this period with them and hope we were all intact on the other end.

She came to me one day and said she needed a break and that she would be taking a week off. I did not hesitate to say I supported her and that she should do what she needs to make sure she stays sane and mentally healthy.

I didn't think much of it at the time. But when I left that company, she mentioned that story at my going-away party. She said she expected it to be a nerve-racking, potentially uncomfortable moment. She knew we were all slammed and that her break would require shifting some of that burden to me. But she said my immediate support of her meant the world.

From CD: After my mom died, I remember struggling in my work a bit. I felt so tormented by this because I felt like I wasn't giving it 100 percent. I brought this up to my manager, and she had so much empathy and compassion for me at that time. She was understanding, and of course reminded me that I wasn't expected to be giving

100 percent, for 100 percent of the time, much less not when I was in the midst of some serious grief.

It meant so much to me that she saw me as a human, not just a worker bee. I felt so supported by her and the whole team, and I really remember the "What can we do to support you?" sentiment—asking me to define how I would work best, if I needed to work from home, et cetera.

When you bring your people with you, everyone wins. But that doesn't mean you (or your team) will never make mistakes. Instead, as you'll see in Chapter 13, leaders worth following learn from both what worked and what didn't.

LEADERS WHO ARE WORTH FOLLOWING... LEARN FROM WHAT WORKED AND WHAT DIDN'T

From K: I had a boss at my previous job who was receptive to hearing feedback but never really acted on it. This was odd because you at once felt like you could tell him how you felt about something he did, but also felt like it was never actually addressed or resolved. It made it feel like we were simply going in circles and became extremely frustrating. It was especially so because the changes and feedback were in an effort to provide for more of my own development.

I eventually left because I didn't think there was much room for me to grow in that company. I had reached what felt like the ceiling.

LEARN FROM YOUR SUCCESSES
AND YOUR MISTAKES

The leaders most worth following are the ones who recognize when they need help and aren't afraid to ask for it. They're also attuned to the times when they get it wrong, and when they do, they always say sorry. When the shoe is on the other foot, they always assume positive intent. They are open to feedback and they listen carefully when they receive it. Doing so means they are better placed to offer feedback when they want to. Learners like to learn from learners.

Feedback is often referred to as "The Breakfast of Champions," but many times the experience of feedback can be more akin to a "Dog's Dinner." As you'll learn in this chapter, being able to perceive the subject of feedback in increasingly more meaningful ways is crucial in the art of giving and receiving it. We'll also discuss how the Theory of Core Qualities provides us with a way of seeing feedback in a positive light.

THE THEORY OF CORE QUALITIES

The Theory of Core Qualities was a model originally designed for HR managers to discuss feedback in a constructive manner. The model suggests four inter-connected positions leading to a quadrant.

THE CORE QUALITY	THE PITFALL
Core Qualities are attributes that form a person's core. Those who know the individual will recognize their Core Qualities immediately. Core Qualities are positive and are considered to be strengths. They are recognized by what others appreciate in you and what you expect/demand from others, and they are often what you downplay in yourself.	Pitfalls exist when an individual exercises too much of a Core Quality. It is the area where most of us get negative feedback. You can recognize areas for your Pitfall by what you are willing to forgive in others and often what you are trying to justify in yourself. The philosophy behind this is that a weakness is not the opposite of a strength but too much of it.
THE ALLERGY	**THE ANTIDOTE**
The Allergy is a reaction to too much of our Challenge and the opposite of the Core Quality. It is what you cannot stand in yourself and in others. You will know it by what you despise in others and what you would hate in yourself if it were present	This is a direct opposite of the Pitfall that, when combined with the Core Quality, keeps you out of the Pitfall, e.g.: a) Determination may need patience so as not to end up as pushiness. b) Loyalty may need objectivity or questioning so as not to become inconsistency. c) Empathy may need self-control to avoid enmeshment. d) Flexibility may need orderliness so as not to become inconsistency.

The four positions are:

- **The Core Quality:** Attributes that form a person's core.

- **The Pitfall:** The area where most of us get negative feedback.

- **The Challenge:** A direct opposite of the Pitfall and combined with the Core Quality keeps individuals out of the Pitfall.

- **The Allergy:** A reaction to too much of our Challenge and the opposite of the Core Quality. It is what I cannot stand in myself and in others.

Here's an example in action:

Miguel is mentor to Prateek. Prateek arrives at his mentoring session troubled by some feedback about being too controlling. This had come up as a theme in his 360 review as something other people needed him to work on.

Miguel explains the Theory of Core Qualities model to Prateek. They agree to put "controlling" into the Pitfall box. Miguel asks him what he does in order for him to be labeled as controlling. Prateek responds immediately. "I am driven to deliver on promises and I like getting things done." They agree that the Core Quality is "delivery."

Miguel then asks Prateek, "If delivery is your Core Quality and controlling is your Pitfall, what is your Antidote?"

Prateek responds immediately, "Bringing people with me," and goes on to say that his Allergy is "letting people down."

Prateek and Miguel now begin to plan for the future and discuss ways in which Prateek can still deliver and get things done while being able to bring people with him. Prateek realizes that to avoid his Pitfall he needs to slow down, agree to different deadlines, and allow other people to take accountability for their work.

It would have been very easy for Prateek to get stuck in the mire of negative feedback and for Miguel to talk to him about the drawbacks of being controlling, but the Theory of Core Qualities gave Prateek an insight into his behavior that did not just concentrate on the negative.

It gave him a way out and a way forward. It provided a constructive platform from which to discuss tools (or Antidotes) to avoid his Pitfall and to balance out his Core Quality.

This does not justify what happens in the Pitfall, but it makes it more easily understood and accepted when placed in a wider context.

THE ART OF GIVING AND RECEIVING FEEDBACK

Another reason why the process of feedback can go so wrong is because when it's given it is laden with mind reads and identity attacks. Let's go back for a moment to the Neurological Levels model in Chapter 6. Through this model, we can clearly see that identity, values and beliefs, capabilities, and behaviors are separate and distinct from each other and occupy a different order of significance to each other.

People will often talk about feedback as being either positive or negative, just as when I'm seeing psychotherapy clients they will often talk about positive and negative emotions. Emotions, just like feedback, are neither positive nor negative in and of themselves.

What makes them positive or negative is the meaning we make out of them. The way we give feedback to someone will influence their meaning-making processes.

I like to use two models for the art of giving feedback: the onion of the self, and the DID model.

THE ONION OF THE SELF

The onion of the self is three concentric circles, with the outer layer representing behavior, the next circle representing values and beliefs, and the inner circle representing identity.

When we look at the onion of the self, it provides us with information to let us know that when we are giving someone feedback, we should only ever stay in that outer layer—behavior. Behavior here is very neatly and tightly described as things you hear other people say and things you see other people do. The layer that is within that, values and beliefs, we can only ever guess at. If we try to give feedback that is about anything other than behavior, we are really mind reading or guessing.

Now, most of us, if asked the question, "Who are you?"

will stumble. Oftentimes we'll answer in terms of the role that we have or things that we do. We'll answer in terms of behavior. Whenever we offer feedback that starts with the words "you are," then that will be immediately received by the other person as a statement of identity. Anytime we say, "I am," "you are," "they are," then we are talking about someone's identity.

But think about the last time you had a tough conversation with a partner or a friend, and you said, "You are such a belligerent asshole." In that example, you are making an accusation about their *identity*. You are not talking about the behavior that leads you to make that judgment about them being a belligerent asshole.

When we say things like, "What I think is going on for you," "I just don't think you value the importance of..." or, "You don't see things in the way that I do," these are all feedback statements at the values and beliefs level—which, again, are not knowable.

So whenever you offer feedback that is an identity-level statement or a values-and-beliefs-level statement, what you're doing is mind reading and what you're gonna get yourself into is an argument.

There's a lovely book called *Counseling for Toads*, which is about transactional analysis that uses the characters from a children's book called *Wind in the Willows*. In *Counseling for Toads*, Toad goes to Badger for counseling, who says to him, "You see, Toad, no one ever changes their mind in an argument. They just get further entrenched in their own views."

If you give feedback at identity level or at values-and-beliefs level, you are moving into a place of argument rather than feedback, because you're going to give rise to heckles and defensiveness. The onion of the self tells us very clearly to stay in behavior, which is things that you heard someone say and things that you saw someone do.

The way to do that is using the DID model, which we'll look at next.

THE DID MODEL

In the DID model, the first D stands for Do, the I stands for Impact, and the second D stands for Differently. This is a very simple model that invites you to curate your feedback around something that you saw or heard the other person *do*, the *impact* of what they did, and then a description of what they can do *differently* next time.

There is a gold version of the DID model, and there's a platinum version of the DID model. The gold version of the DID model is exactly as I stated: telling someone what they did, what the impact was, and what you'd like them to do differently next time. The platinum version of the DID model is telling them what they did, and then asking *them* to consider what the impact was and what they would do differently next time.

As an example, let's say DDS and Dear Reader (DR) are in a meeting together, and DR is typing on their laptop. Now a really bad way of giving identity- or values-and-beliefs-level feedback would be to say, "DR, you were on your laptop during that entire meeting. You don't care about the client. It was just rude." (As I said, bad feedback. Just don't do that.)

The gold version of the DID model would be to say, "DR, I noticed in that meeting that you were on your laptop while the client was speaking." That is a behavior-level statement; it's undeniable that DR was on their laptop while the client was speaking. And then I would say, "The problem with that is the client might think you are not interested in what they've got to say, and they might not think they're very important. So next time, what I would like you to do is either bring a notepad into the meeting instead of your laptop, or let the client know you are taking notes so they don't think you are checking your emails or responding to chats."

The platinum version would be, "DR, I noticed in that meeting that you were working on your laptop while the client was speaking. Can you share a little bit about what you think the impact might have been on the client?"

DR would say, "Well, I was taking notes on the meeting."

And I might say, "Yeah, I understand that. But the client didn't know that. So what do you think the impact on the client would be?"

DR would say, "I dunno, maybe they thought I was being rude. Maybe they thought I didn't care. Maybe they thought I was doing other work."

"Yeah, all of that is possible. So what could you do differently next time?"

"Maybe instead of my laptop, I could bring a notepad in or better still, maybe at the beginning of the meeting, I could let the client know I'm going to take minutes or I'm going to take notes using my laptop."

The DID model is a really beautiful way of offering feedback that doesn't get you into an argument and doesn't cause defensiveness.

THE ART OF RECEIVING FEEDBACK

The extent to which your people will receive feedback will be correlated to the way feedback is given. There is an art not only to giving feedback, but also to receiving feedback.

There are four rules for receiving feedback in an artful way.

I. **Practice active listening.** While receiving feedback, maintain good eye contact. Think about your physiology. Does your body show that you are listening? Listen with the intent to understand rather than the intent to respond. Don't interrupt. Perhaps summarize what you've heard and then ask any clarifying questions—and they have to be questions of genuine curiosity and clarification, rather than opinions masquerading as questions.

2. **Never argue. Just say thank you.** Some people have a tendency to turn clarifying questions into some form of spirited defense, and that's just going to stop the other person from ever offering you feedback again (which may be the intended effect!). There is only one appropriate response to constructive feedback, which is just to say thank you. "Thank you for bringing this to my attention. Thank you for sharing it with me. I will chew on this and would it be okay if I came back to you if I have any more questions?"

3. **Evaluate it slowly.** Get in the practice of reflecting on feedback for a day or more. Check in with yourself. Does the criticism seem true? Is it something you already knew was a limitation? The other thing to remember is that feedback isn't about your likability. It isn't about whether you are a good person or not; it's about the impact of your behavior.

4. **Stay mindful.** Look for opportunities to stop or start doing the critiqued behaviors. If, after you have tried out new behaviors or stopped old behav-

iors, you feel you are better off for receiving the feedback given by the other person, don't forget to go back to that person to let them know their feedback helped.

BOUNCE-BACK-ABILITY

A wise person once said, "It is not the falling down that matters but the manner in which we rise afterwards that counts." When a leader recognizes that they are a work in progress and that they don't know everything, they are more able to ask for help when they need it, or accept it when it's offered and they aren't perhaps aware that they need it. They know this is a sign of strength, not weakness.

Resilience, or bounce-back-ability (BBA) as I like to call it, is a necessary component of the sur-*thrival* kit of any leader, not only because all that we knew to be normal at work has been turned upside down and on its head but also because it works hand in hand with the value of **tenacity**.[23]

---

23 A topic we wrote about in an article entitled "Just Keep Swimming, Dory" is available here: https://soul-trained.medium.com/just-keep-swimming-dory-1bf705bf3ed3.

We often hear leaders talking about the way in which they "survived the day," "made it through," or "scraped by" in challenging times, but we want to aim higher. I believe that it is possible to not only survive the bumps, knocks, and inevitable missteps of leadership life, but that it is possible to sail through them, to rise *because* of them, or to become more resilient as a result of them.

First, let's get a handle on what an absence of bounce-back-ability might look like. Start by asking yourself these questions:

- Can I easily return to a state of calm and center in times of stress?

- Am I able to metabolize my upsets and channel them toward constructive outcomes?

- Do I adapt well to rapidly changing contexts and conditions?

- Do I handle setbacks and mistakes with grace and in the spirit of growth?

- Do I believe that there is no such thing as failure, that there is just information and feedback?

- Can I leave the past in the past, or do I ruminate?

- Do I invest in regular practices that build my physical, emotional, and mental health?

- Do I access support backup when I hit emotional overload?

If you answered no, or if you were unsure of how to answer any of the questions above, then read on.

Take a look at this list of behaviors and habits. In my work with leaders who are working on their bounce-back-ability, I often find these cropping up:

- You have a difficult time saying no to requests and demands on your time when your plate is already full.

- It is hard for you to see the forest for the trees, and you often struggle to prioritize between what's important to you and what is important to others.

- After a difficult conversation you dwell on it and keep turning it over in your mind.

- You work in a competitive culture and sacrifice periodic reflection for constant action.

- You experience little control or choice over your work or what assignments you take on.

- You often sacrifice empathy for toughness.

- Your self-reliance keeps you from trusting others.

- You overrely only on existing strengths and stay away from situations that require you to flex new muscles or develop new skills.

Do any of them seem familiar to you? If so, it's likely time to start developing and nurturing your BBA.

How? Well, it takes, in the words of Dr. Chris Shambrook,[24] self-awareness, self-acceptance, and self-improvement (in that order).

---

24 I chatted with him for an episode of the *Shift Happens* podcast, titled "Let Go and Let Lead Coaching," available here: https://soultrained.com/podcast/let-go-lead-coaching/

SELF-AWARENESS

I concur with Simon Sinek, who wrote *Start with Why*, and Laura van Dernoot Lipsky, who wrote *Trauma Stewardship*, both of whom encourage us to develop an awareness of and connection with the reasons why we do what we do, and connect our work to the achievements of a bigger goal in life.

As Lipsky says, "This will help us to alleviate the sensation of being tossed around in the waves of uncontrollable and overwhelming events."

Syndee Brooker, a participant in a leadership workshop I was running recently, casually dropped the following line into the Zoom chat window: "Work will always fill the container you give it," and I couldn't agree more. How aware are you of the shape, size, and capacity of your "work container"?

Balance

Many people talk about regaining work–life balance as a form of building resilience, but I have a different take on the topic, preferring instead to encourage our clients to think about **work–life blend** instead (a concept I'll come back to shortly).

It might be that I am one of those people who has a strong connection between my **identity and my work** (my work is part of who I am, rather than something I do). It might also be because I am observing my husband working evenings, weekends, and daytimes to keep up with their workload.

Whichever it is, I've been thinking a lot about work–life balance recently. In fact I've been wondering whether there is actually such a thing at all (don't worry, this ends on a good note).

So I wanted to take a moment to pause, take stock, and reflect on it.

It is a well-known fact that ad agency work requires long hours. While it's true that this is most definitely not an industry for those who want a nine-to-five, I agree with the sentiment of the article "The Culture of Long Agency Hours" by Jack Marshall, which argues that rest is a prerequisite for high performance.[25] I believe it's time to challenge the fact and perhaps start to see that what we have come to accept as fact is actually a phenomenon that may not need to be true.

---

25   Marshall, "The Culture of Long Agency Hours."

Let's talk about **balance** for a moment. Given that a week contains 168 hours, can there ever really be *balance*? Would you really want to spend eighty-four hours at work (let's set aside the legislation that exists around the world limiting the working week to somewhere between thirty-five and forty hours) and another eighty-four hours of not at work?

I've never worked anywhere where employees have said, "Yep, we're good. We've got enough people to cover the amount of work that we do!" Not even in civil service where the staffing budgets tend to be more generous than in Fortune 500 or FTSE 100 companies. There will never be enough people. The work will never be fully done. There is always a presentation to tweak, a report to optimize, another conversation to be had, or a bar to be raised. But at what cost? At whose expense?

So, surely it isn't about striking a balance at all!

Could it perhaps be more about becoming more conscious of how you prioritize your time while at work? Or could it be about becoming more aware of the choices you make to stay connected with work when you leave the office—about how you leave work at work, or not?

I know it isn't always that simple. We all have coworkers, clients, customers, deadlines, and deliverables. Equally we all have the same twenty-four hours in the day. But it is **this very simple and very impactful article** by Adam Dachis—with the life hack in the title "Instead of Saying 'I Don't Have Time,' Say 'It's Not a Priority'"—that reminded me of the choices I make every moment of every day in terms of how I spend my twenty-four hours.[26]

When was the last time you checked in on the choices you're making? Where do you place yourself on your list of priorities?

Human Doings

Recently I began to notice a theme emerge when I asked people how they were (I'm one of those people who asks the question because I really am interested in your answer). I noticed that the first words to come in response to my inquiry were, "I'm busy," or some variation on that theme. I began to notice the dissonance between inquiring after someone's well-being and being told about what they're doing.

---

26 Dachis, "Instead of Saying 'I Don't Have Time.'"

Sometimes I wonder whether we forget how to not be busy, to not be stressed, to not work all the hours that the universe needs us to. I think this happens because the choices we make from our default map of the world feel right to us simply because they're familiar. But when the odd late night or early morning extends over a period of time, unless we remember to pump the brakes a little, we become comfortable in the new version of the game we are playing, and it becomes the new normal. And so the cycle repeats. We just get busier and busier and busier.

We all experience self-doubt and feelings of inadequacy. Louise Hay would even say that the bottom line for each of us is that we are not good enough. If this is true, I wonder sometimes whether we keep ourselves stuck in the pattern of being busy to counteract the bottom line—to cancel out our feelings of inadequacy, to feel good enough.

Are we beginning to forget that we're human *beings*, not human *doings*? I wonder who we'd be if we weren't so busy doing. I wonder if we did less, what we'd become. Perhaps we could work on our self-belief and begin to find that our worthiness is not attached to our productivity.

Work to Live or Live to Work?

I'm a high-achieving control freak in recovery. I'm a work in progress (as are we all).

I still fall off the wagon every now and again, but before my days of earnest recovery, a friend once said to me, "Are you living to work, DDS, or are you working to live?"

I think my reply then was the same as how I would reply if she asked me today: "Both."

The way in which the phrase "work–life balance" is constructed might lead us into the false perception that there is work and there is life and that the two are separate; that anything that isn't work is life and that anything that isn't life is work. But I don't believe this to be true.

I believe work is a part of life and that life is so much more than just not-work. You only have to take a look at the popular coaching tool the Wheel of Life[27] to see that work is just one aspect of life. Work is a part of life, not an alternative to it. Work is something you do while being alive, having a life, or doing life.

27   Baker, "Wheel of Life."

New and emerging technologies have led to a blurring of the boundaries and definition of "workplace." Sure there is still the need for human contact (especially in client-related work) and the need to be present to be a good colleague or leader, but working from somewhere other than the office premises provided by the company for which you work is no longer a necessity 24/7.

In this context, perhaps there is no such thing as work–life balance. Perhaps we can begin to conceive of a concept of Life Management, or even work–life blending instead of work–life balance. If I think about work–life blending, I feel more empowered. In work-life blending, you are in the driver's seat and fully aware of the choices you are making and where in your Important List you are placing yourself.

Imagine a scenario in which you are able to deftly blend all aspects of your life so that they work harmoniously for you and the way you want to live your life.

Self-Acceptance

Allow yourself to notice that you are a human being, not a human doing; you are always doing the best you can with the resources, tools, and time you have available to you. Even though the environments we work in try to hoodwink us into believing otherwise, your self-worth is not tied to your productivity.

The title of this book, *Leadership Is a Behavior, Not a Title,* in and of itself is a useful reminder that how you show up in your job can often be more important than what you deliver in your job.

Whenever you take a plane, during the safety announcements before taking off, they tell you about the oxygen masks that will fall from the ceiling in the event of the air pressure in the cabin changing. They always tell you to put your own mask on before helping others. Have you ever thought about why they say that?

If we were to apply the same logic to the workplace, then we might make some new and different decisions about the extent to which we take care of ourselves before taking care of others (NB: in our recent polls, "showing genuine care for others" was the top-ranked leadership behavior that people are motivated by). Whether you are restored by a hike in the woods, a sweaty workout in the gym, reading a good book, or brunch with close friends, it is crucial that you develop a wellness ritual...and stick to it. Your resilience will thank you for it. We promise.

SELF-DEVELOPMENT

It is a fallacy that the leader has (or has to have) all the answers. Similarly, the concept of "making it" is false. You will never "arrive" because you are a work in progress, and you always will be. The thing about works in progress is that they only really progress when they work on their progress. In other words, your development won't happen by accident.

With this in mind, we cannot emphasize enough the importance of cultivating a support team. Finding a mentor, an advocate, and/or a coach is part of that. But so is, as Buckingham and Coffman remind us, having a best friend at work—not the kind of bestie who colludes with you and tells you what you want to hear, but the kind of bestie who will tell you a few home truths when you need them. This underscores the important role leaders play in facilitating social relationships across their teams.

Beyond the learning that comes from a support team, off-the-job learning through workshops, programs, and certifications will build your capability. In doing so, it will grow your capacity for complexity and therefore feed your bounce-back-ability.

Ask yourself about the steps you have taken recently to develop a new skill, acquire new knowledge, and expand your capability. Is it time? And, if you don't know what skill or knowledge to build, tap into your Why (to bring this full circle) to understand what type of development might be most beneficial to your personal and professional direction of travel.

EXAMPLES OF THE IMPORTANCE OF LEARNING FROM WHAT WORKED AND WHAT DIDN'T

From JW: I came to Canada fifteen years ago, and my previous boss cared for his staff and would listen and learn.

Since being here, I have dealt with bosses who blame others, don't take feedback, and keep doing the same thing even when it causes problems. There could be many reasons for this, but my theory has been that when the performance has met your superiors' expectations, you are okay. When people talk about culture starting at the top, it really does make sense because otherwise there is no incentive.

From AH: Ego will get you nowhere, and one can only "fake it till they make it" for so long. A vulnerable manager or teammate is actually one easier to collaborate with.

From XH: A growth mindset is a must for a person in a leadership position. I have seen a leader who could not appreciate how much another person can grow and improve. Also, the same leader could not read the changing situation well and be adaptive enough to be really effective.

From AS: I remember very young in my career not being listened to because I was junior, yet I could clearly see the problem and how to fix it. It was frustrating as my manager wouldn't give me time, let alone listen, and because I was junior I didn't have the confidence to speak up. Seniority doesn't always mean you have all the answers so it's important to be open to suggestions from all angles and individuals.

One of the things I remind my team is that I am human, I will make mistakes, and I don't have all the answers—but together we can overcome. Always approach with empathy and a solutions-oriented mindset to get through something together, learn from each other, and realize everyone can help. I don't see titles, I see people, and each one is equal.

CONCLUSION

The first time I really understood the impact a great leader can make was when I got what I referred to as my first "grown-up job," as head of organizational development at Eurostar, a travel company that runs passenger trains between central London and continental Europe.

For one of my roles there, I reported to the HR director. The HR director who recruited me moved on to a new job, and a new director was appointed. He had no experience in HR. None. He was a customer-service person. In fact, before he became the HR director, he was the customer-service director. Many people were shocked and surprised when he moved into the role, some pleasantly, some less so.

I knew him because we'd worked together in a different capacity before he came into this role. And I remember him saying to me, "I have absolutely no idea how to do your job. I don't know what it is. I don't have the skill. I don't have the expertise. And therefore, I don't know how to help you from a technical point of view. But what I can do is support you and enable you to be the best you can be in your job. So, can you tell me what that looks like for you?"

And in that moment—when this person revealed his vulnerability and courageously said, "I haven't got a clue how to do what you do," and very clearly stated that he believed that it was his job to help me to achieve my objectives, not my job to help him achieve his objectives—in that very moment, I bought into him. I would have followed him over a cliff.

That was a role-model relationship for me because he made it his job to make me successful. Now, he did it in a way that ensured there were some guardrails. I wasn't just off doing my own thing; he helped connect me into the business—the strategy of the business and the direction of the business—but he wanted to take what it was that I did and help me to be even better at it.

I didn't have those six principles in front of me (how could I? I hadn't written them yet), but he was absolutely somebody who maybe didn't have the exact words of these six principles but who embodied them nonetheless.

That was a leader worth following.

IT STARTS WITH YOU

I hope this book has been a mirror that you can hold up to yourself and determine where your gaps may be and where your growth can come from. That's the self-awareness piece.

The job of self-acceptance is now up to you. If you've had the courage to take a look in the mirror that this book provides, I want you to notice the ideas and concepts with which you experience the most resistance or those that you want to push back on most vehemently. Those are likely to be the areas of greatest growth and greatest gain you can have.

And once you have noticed and become aware of your gaps, and are fully owning those gaps, then you are able to move into self-development. What does that look like? Of course I would encourage you to have a support team, whether that's a coach, a mentor, or an advocate.

Recognize that the job of becoming increasingly human and increasingly someone who is worth following isn't a job that is ever complete. We are not a finished product and we never will be. We don't get to graduate from personal growth.

If you are interested in learning more, I also run a leadership growth training called ENRICH, which is built around the Six Principles of Human Leadership you've read about here. It involves a range of experiences—including virtual workshops, peer-to-peer learning, and one-on-one learning—which work in concert to offer participants a growth experience that is practical, reflective, and deeply meaningful, personally and professionally.

LEADERSHIP IS NECESSARY NOW

The world needs more leaders who are worth following more than ever before.

We are being constantly surprised and let down by

people in power, by our institutions and governments, by people we've voted for and those we haven't. And still we are surprised and let down by them.

It's disheartening. It is disorienting. It is dysregulating and harmful, and it is painful.

Having role models we can look up to and be inspired by—people we can see ourselves reflected back through, people who are consistent, available, and *human*—can create psychological safety. In a world where our psychological safety can feel threatened on the daily, having more leaders who are worth following couldn't be more topical.

Leaders who are worth following bring us stability, instill hope, and bolster our confidence. They help us believe we can do the hard things.

What we need now is more togetherness. And leaders who are worth following, who live out these Six Principles of Human Leadership, rather than exclude and cause division—they integrate, include, and inspire.

The good news is there isn't one way to be a leader worth following; there's just *your* way. With increasing levels of humanity and self-awareness, self-acceptance, and self-development, the way that you are a leader is the perfect way to be a leader.

This book hasn't put forward a step-by-step equation for how to be a great leader, but I hope that it has offered food for thought, frameworks, tools, resources, and stories that will help you reflect on where you are, in regard to the extent to which you might be deemed worthy of being followed by other people. I hope you are able to recognize that being a leader worth following is about being yourself, but with increasing amounts of skill, behavioral flexibility, and conscious choice.

The ideas and concepts that are put forward in this book are not a silver bullet. They are not a magic potion, and there's no wand I can wave to bestow leadership upon you. But you can continue to grow, and you can come back to what you've learned here when the journey of being a leader worth following becomes bumpy, as journeys inevitably do. I hope that these concepts have provided some suspension for the wheels, padding for the seat, and oil for the machinery.

Here, at the end of this particular journey, I want you to

stop asking yourself, "How do I become a great leader?" and *start* asking, "How do I become someone worth following?"

BIBLIOGRAPHY

Baker, Brendan. "Wheel of Life—A Self-Assessment Tool." The Start of Happiness. Accessed August 2, 2022. https://www.startofhappiness.com/wheel-of-life-a-self-assessment-tool.

Berne, Eric. *Games People Play: The Psychology of Human Relationships*. New York: Grove Press, 1964.

Bridges, William. *Managing Transitions: Making the Most of Change*. Boston: Da Capo Lifelong Books, 1991.

Buckingham, Marcus. *First, Break All the Rules: What the World's Greatest Managers Do Differently*. New York, NY: Simon & Schuster, 1999.

Charan, Ram, Stephen Drotter, and James Noel. *The Leadership Pipeline: How to Build the Leadership Powered Company*. Hoboken, NJ: Jossey-Bass, 2011.

Charvet, Shelle Rose. *Words That Change Minds: The 14 Patterns for Mastering the Language of Influence*. Wilmington, DE: Bloomanity LLC, 2019.

Covey, Stephen R. *The 7 Habits of Highly Effective People: Powerful Lessons in Personal Change*. New York: Free Press, 1990

Csikszentmihalyi, Mihaly. *Flow: The Psychology of Optimal Experience*. New York: Harper & Row, 1990.

Dachis, Adam. "Instead of Saying 'I Don't Have Time,' Say 'It's Not a Priority.'" LifeHacker, March 13, 2012. http://lifehacker.com/5892948/instead-of-saying-i-dont-have-time-say-its-not-a-priority.

De Board, Robert. *Counselling for Toads: A Psychological Adventure*. London: Routledge, 1997.

Dobson-Smith, DDS. *You Can Be Yourself Here: Your Pocket Guide to Creating Inclusive Workplaces by Using the Psychology of Belonging*. Austin, TX: Lioncrest Publishing, 2022.

Frankl, Viktor. *Man's Search for Meaning: An Introduction to Logotherapy*. Boston: Beacon Press, 1962.

Goffee, Robert and Gareth Jones. "Why Should Anyone Be Led by You?" *Harvard Business Review*, September–October 2000. https://hbr.org/2000/09/why-should-anyone-be-led-by-you.

Goffee, Robert and Gareth Jones. *Why Should Anyone Be Led by You?: What It Takes to Be an Authentic Leader*. Cambridge, MA: Harvard Business Review Press, 2006.

Hougaard, Rasmus. "The Real Crisis in Leadership." *Forbes*, September 9, 2018. https://www.forbes.com/sites/rasmushougaard/2018/09/09/the-real-crisis-in-leadership.

James, Tad and Wyatt Woodsmall. *Time Line Therapy and the Basis of Personality*. Chicago: Meta Publications, 1989.

Karpman, Stephen B. "Fairy Tales and Script Drama Analysis." *Transactional Analysis Bulletin* 7, no. 26 (1968): 39-43.

Kelly, George. *The Psychology of Personal Constructs*. New York: W.W. Norton & Company, 1955.

Kübler-Ross, Elisabeth. *On Death and Dying: What the Dying Have to Teach Doctors, Nurses, Clergy, and Their Own Families*. New York: Simon & Schuster, 1970.

Marshall, Jack. "The Culture of Long Agency Hours." *Digiday*, Februrary 12, 2013. https://digiday.com/marketing/the-culture-of-long-agency-hours.

Mehrabian, Albert. *Silent Messages*. Belmont, CA: Wadsworth Publishing Co., 1971.

Re: Work. *Guide: Understand Team Effectiveness*. Google. Accessed August 2, 2022. https://rework.withgoogle.com/print/guides/5721312655835136.

Rogers, Carl R. *A Way of Being: The Founder of the Human Potential Movement Looks Back on a Distinguished Career*. New York: Houghton Mifflin, 1980.

Sinek, Simon. *Start With Why: How Great Leaders Inspire Everyone to Take Action*. New York: Portfolio, 2009.

Soul Trained. "'Just Keep Swimming.' Dory." Medium, June 29, 2021. https://soul-trained.medium.com/just-keep-swimming-dory-1bf705bf3ed3.

Soul Trained. "De-fearing Your Fear: Making Vulnerability Your Greatest Asset." Medium, September 28, 2021. https://soul-trained.medium.com/de-fearing-your-fear-making-vulnerability-your-greatest-asset-27fb48d440f7.

Van Dernoot Lipsky, Laura, with Connie Burk. *Trauma Stewardship: An Everyday Guide to Caring for Self While Caring for Others*. Oakland, CA: Berrett-Koehler Publishers, 2009.

Waite, Terry. "How I Survived 5 Years of Torture." Interview by Holly Willoughby and Philip Schofield. *This Morning*, February 12, 2016. https://www.youtube.com/watch?v=ZilDoOtkJ6g.

Zimmerman, Allyson. "Teams Grow Stronger When Managers Show Openness and Vulnerability." *LSE Business Review* (blog). The London School of Economics and Political Science, July 22, 2021. https://blogs.lse.ac.uk/businessreview/2021/07/22/teams-grow-stronger-when-managers-show-openness-and-vulnerability.

ABOUT ME

I'm a queer, nonbinary, nondisabled, white British immigrant who was assigned male at birth, and I have lived in the US with my husband, Davis, and our two Maine coon cats—Harper and Hemingway—since 2014.

After eight years of living in the Bay Area, in January of 2022, Davis, Harper, Hemingway, and I moved to Connecticut, where you'll find me taking great joy in the transitions of the seasons. I love losing myself in repeats of *The Voice*, *American Idol*, *Got Talent*, and *The X Factor* on YouTube or keeping up with the *RuPaul's Drag Race* seasons that seem to now run concurrently around the world.

I bring all of my experiences as a human and my training as a clinician and a coach to show up in my authenticity, genuineness, and truth and to approach my work and my clinical practice in a person-centered, trauma-informed, culturally humble way.

A beloved teacher of mine once told me that our goal in life is to become increasingly better at being at odds with ourselves, and I felt that to be true deep in my soul. I notice that accepting this to be true and welcoming this into one's experience requires shift: shifts in the way we think and feel, the way we make meaning from our experiences, and the way in which we show up for our Self, other Selves, and within life itself.

I believe that true shift happens through a process of hard human kindness, of immense empathy, and love along with a good dollop of nerve and candor. I also believe that shift happens most sustainably—and alchemically—through a greater acceptance of, and connection with, the person you really are; when you are fully you—your youest you—life, and everything in it, can be gorgeous, fulfilling, and joyful. Each of these philosophies underpin my approach and my work.

I have notched up over twenty-five years of working in

small, medium, and large corporations. I literally grew up in the hospitality industry (my parents owned a pub and restaurant in the UK), and I started my career as a college professor teaching hotel and business management. I've since held a range of senior, executive, and C-suite-level roles across a host of sectors and companies, including retailer Marks & Spencer PLC, travel and tourism company Eurostar International, Crossrail Ltd.—the company charged with building a new railway through the center of London—music giant Sony Music Entertainment, and Essence Global—part of the world's largest advertising company, WPP. These roles have provided the opportunity for me to work across all continents and to develop the awareness and empathy required to work successfully with people from all walks of life and diverse backgrounds. Today, I am the founder and CEO of Soul Trained, a consultancy firm that is on a mission to fill the world full of leaders who are worth following and create workplaces where people can be themselves.

I'm certified as an Executive Coach by both the Chartered Institute of Personnel and Development and the Oxford School of Coaching & Mentoring. I'm credentialed with the International Coach Federation, and I am a coach-supervisor through the Coaching Supervision Academy. In 2018, I founded Soul Trained, an executive coaching and leadership growth consultancy, and in February 2022 I published my first book, *You Can Be Yourself Here: Your Pocket Guide to Creating Inclusive Workplaces Using the Psychology of Belonging,* which quickly became a number one bestseller.

Before I moved to the US in 2014, I managed a small psychotherapy private practice as a licensed neuro linguistic psychotherapist. Neuro linguistic psychotherapy has its roots in a body of work known as neuro linguistic programming, which was founded in the 1970s by Richard Bandler (a mathematician, computer programmer, and therapist) and John Grinder (a world-renowned linguist).

Bandler and Grinder were heavily influenced by the Human Potential Movement and by Gregory Bateson (anthropologist, social scientist, linguist, and systems thinker), Fritz and Laura Perls (the founders of Gestalt psychotherapy), Virginia Satir (family therapist), and Milton Erickson (psychiatrist, family therapist, and founding president of the American Society for Clinical Hypnosis). While NLPt certainly developed from this body of work, NLPt practitioners trace the roots of the field even further back to Alfred Korzybski's notion that "the map is not the territory," to George Kelly's *Psychology of Personal Constructs*, and to the work of George A. Miller, the cognitive scientist.

Between 2002 and 2022, I worked as both a clinician and as the Board President at Pacific Center for Human Growth in Berkley, the country's second-oldest community mental health clinic serving the needs of the LGBTQIA2+ community, which centers on mental health as a social justice issue. Through my work at Pacific Center I have learned to value the question, "What happened to you?" versus wondering, "What's wrong with you?" and to appreciate the many ways in which systemic racism, sexism, ableism, and heterosexism impact our emotional, mental, and physical health.

In addition to my training and licensure in the UK, in 2021 I graduated from California Institute of Integral Studies with an MA in integral counseling psychology. As a student of integral counseling psychology, over the years I've had the opportunity to train with, and learn from, many luminaries in the transpersonal field including Louise Hay (author of *You Can Heal Your Life*), Marianne Williamson (author of *A Return to Love*), Dr. Patricia Crane (author of *Ordering from the*

Cosmic Kitchen), and Jason Chan (author of *The Radiant Warrior*). In 2007, I became a reiki master and teacher under the guidance of Christina Moore. In 2019, I completed an internship with the Narrative Enneagram, and in 2021 I completed another internship as a crystal bowl sound healer with Shalom Mayberg. In August 2022, I embarked on a new journey of personal and professional growth when I began a PhD in human sexuality at California Institute of Integral Studies.

In addition to my consultancy, Soul Trained, I run a private psychotherapy practice called Soul*Full* therapy in Newtown, Connecticut. I help adult survivors of chaotic childhoods to heal the parts of themselves that hold the pain of their past so that they may live more fully in the here and now. As a member of the LGBTQIA2+ community myself, I also work with cis and trans people (youth and adults) who are journeying through gender identity, gender expression, and coming-out issues. I am a relational therapist and practice through a social-justice-informed and feminist frame. My thinking is informed by neurolinguistic psychotherapy, psychodynamic psychotherapy, Gestalt psychotherapy, and internal family systems.

CPSIA information can be obtained
at www.ICGtesting.com
Printed in the USA
BVHW052020200922
647265BV00004B/18